# GARDENERS' WORLD
## BOOK OF
# CONTAINER GARDENING
## ANNE SWITHINBANK

# GARDENERS' WORLD

# BOOK OF

# CONTAINER GARDENING

## ANNE SWITHINBANK

BBC BOOKS

## ACKNOWLEDGEMENTS

*Special thanks to the following:*
Anna Martin, plant consultant, 60 Beauchamp Road,
Upper Norwood, London SE19 3BD, tel. 081-771 6623,
for tracking down plants and containers and planting them up;
Capel Manor Horticultural and Environmental Centre,
Bullsmoor Lane, Enfield, Middlesex EN1 4RQ for making their facilities available,
caring for and planting up some of the containers;
and in particular, Miranda Townsend-Coles and David Grigg.
Jacques Amand, bulb specialists,
The Nurseries, Clamp Hill,
Stanmore, Middlesex HA7 3JS.

Published by BBC Books,
a division of BBC Enterprises Limited,
Woodlands, 80 Wood Lane, London W12 0TT

First published 1992

ISBN 0 563 36129 8

Photographs by Norman Brand
Set in 10/12½ pt Kennerley by Ace Filmsetting Ltd, Frome
Printed and bound in Great Britain by Clays Ltd, St Ives Plc
Colour separations by Dot Gradations Ltd, Berkhamsted
Cover printed by Clays Ltd, St Ives Plc

# CONTENTS

# TUBS, URNS, TROUGHS AND POTS

Growing plants in containers, although certainly not a new idea, seems tailor made for the sort of gardening we enjoy today. Many of us only have small gardens and confining plants to containers may be the best, and most exciting, choice available. Also, when anticipating a short stay in a property, container-grown plants will be easy to move on.

In larger gardens, terraces and patios can be brightened by containers planted for different seasons. Potfuls of bedding plants, lilies, foliage plants or spring bulbs can be placed in parts of the garden going through a dull patch. A narrow garden will look wider if the eye is drawn across rather than down, and one way of achieving this is to place an urn bursting with vivid colour to one side, perhaps emphasising the curve of a sinuous path. Climbers can be grown up buildings where there are no soil beds. I have grown a beautiful *Fremontodendron californicum* in a large half-barrel against a south-facing wall which rewards us with masses of yellow flowers every summer.

Both containers and plants are expensive, so it makes sense to choose well and take good care of them. Make sure there are adequate drainage holes in the base of the container. Not only does waterlogging create problems for plant roots but the container itself will be more vulnerable to frost damage when excess moisture in the compost freezes and expands in winter. Always look for terracotta pots that are sold as frost proof but even these must be cared for. This means adequate crocking of the base with broken pots, expanded clay pebbles or shingle. Raising the container off the ground may be necessary to allow free escape of water. Never use ordinary garden soil as it can become too compact.

The current trend is away from using too much peat for conservation reasons. I have not had the opportunity to test the peat-alternative composts in containers and so fight shy of recommending them. I have, however, always had good results from John Innes No. 2 or 3 compost, with added peat for its fibrous nature, and grit or sharp sand to improve drainage of water. I also mix together equal quantities of John Innes and peat-based composts. Although possibly frowned on professionally, this mixture works well for me.

Having chosen plants carefully so that they will look good together, complement the container, suit the position you have in mind and perform in the season you require, then make sure you water them regularly, and be prepared to feed the plants more than if they were in a border. Liquid fertiliser diluted in water is the commonest method, especially for bedding plants. For shrubs I prefer to use a spring application of slow-release fertiliser designed to last the entire growing season.

**PLANT**
One umbrella pine (*Sciadopitys verticillata*).

**CONTAINER** Spanish terracotta pot measuring 15 inches (38 cm) high and 17 inches (43 cm) diameter.

**POSITION** Sun or semi-shade. Avoid a windswept position.

**W**hereas some pines, restricted to a container, become untidy and lose needles, their close relative *Sciadopitys* remains a tidy and attractive specimen. This plant has lived in its container in a south-, then a west-facing, position for four years and has been much admired.

Bought in a pot, the umbrella pine can be planted up at any time. As it dislikes waterlogged soil, place a good layer of expanded clay pebbles or crocks in the bottom of the pot before filling in with compost. Use a mixture prepared for acid-loving plants. Keep moist during summer and top dress with a slow-release fertiliser like Vitax Q4 for trees and shrubs in spring.

A native of Japan, *Sciadopitys* reaches 120 feet (37 m) in its forest home. Early growth progresses very slowly so young plants will long remain suitable for a container. Of the true pines, probably *Pinus mugo pumilio*, the dwarf mountain pine, is the most suited to a container. This European pine is unlikely to grow more than 6 feet (1.8 m) high but can have a branched, spreading habit and will eventually need some space. The variety 'Gnom' is more compact. Wayward branches can be pruned off and this is a useful specimen for a colder, more windswept site than *Sciadopitys* would withstand. *Pinus sylvestris*, the Scots pine, would grow far too quickly but *P. sylvestris* 'Beuvronensis' only reaches a hummocky 3 feet (91 cm) with short, grey-green leaves. I prefer more graceful pines and would choose *Pinus parviflora* 'Glauca', a slow grower with wonderful blue needles. As it has a more open shape, it can be tidied up by pruning off unwanted branches. *Pinus strobus*, the Weymouth pine, has a dwarf form *P.s.* 'Nana'. A rounded 3 to 6 feet (91 cm to 1.8 m), this has long, soft grey-green needles. For a Christmas-tree shaped conifer, choose *Abies koreana*, the Korean fir. This, although it would normally reach about 30 feet (9 m) in height, will stay small when restricted to a container and will produce its dark, violet-blue cones when as small as 3 feet (91 cm).

The Lawson cypress, *Chamaecyparis lawsoniana*, is well known but far too rapid a grower to be comfortably restricted to a container for long. However, its dwarf forms are most suitable. *C.l.* 'Elwoodii' has attractive blue-grey leaves. *Chamaecyparis pisifera* 'Boulevard', a variety of the Sawara cypress, will remain small. This is most attractive, having a soft, feathery appearance with silvery bluish-green leaves. The slightest drying out at the roots, particularly in the case of 'Boulevard', will result in ugly brown patches forming at the base of the plant. These never recover and subsequent dry periods will only worsen the trouble, so regular and thorough summer (and winter if necessary) waterings are the rule.

**PLANTS**

1 One dwarf rhododendron
   (*Rhododendron yakushimanum*).
2 Ten clumps of *Galanthus caucasicus*
   (snowdrops).

**CONTAINER** Spanish terracotta bowl
measuring 9 inches (23 cm) high and 18
inches (46 cm) diameter.

**POSITION** Semi-shade is preferred.

One of the benefits of container growing
is that regardless of whether your garden
soil is acid or alkaline, light or heavy, you
can tailor the compost used to suit any
type of plant. This is particularly important
with plants which need acid soils, as many
of them are of great ornamental value, yet
without their preferred soil it is hardly
worth the trouble and expense of planting
them. Rhododendrons fit into this category. While the taller-growing kinds
would eventually begin to feel restricted,
reflecting this in their appearance, there
are plenty of dwarf types to choose from
which thrive well in tubs and pots.

Theoretically, a pot-grown plant can be
bought and planted at any time of the year.
I would favour spring or autumn, definitely
spring if you are going to include the
snowdrops. Crock the base with broken
clay pots or expanded clay pebbles. Plant
the rhododendron into ericaceous compost, making sure not to plant either
deeper or higher than the top of the
rootball. Ideally there should be just a
sprinkling of new compost over the old
surface. The best way of establishing the
snowdrops, ordinary *G. nivalis* will do, is
to buy them 'in the green', that is, after
they have flowered and their leaves are
more in evidence. Even better, scrounge
them from a friend's garden, lifting and
dividing old clumps when they have finished flowering. Plant these under the rhododendron in the same season to avoid
later root disturbance. Should you decide
to make an underplanting of crocus, or
other sorts of bulbs more successful from
an autumn planting, then plant the rhododendron at the same time. I have found it
beneficial to cover the compost surface
with a layer of expanded clay pebbles. This
keeps new compost in place during rain-
storms, stops cats from digging, helps
retain moisture and, to an extent, shelters
the roots from hot sun.

Keeping the compost moist, particularly
during summer, is crucial to the well-being
and performance of the plant. One or two
occasions of drying out may well not kill
the rhododendron but will probably stop it
from flowering the following May. Give a
spring top-dressing of slow-release
fertiliser formulated for acid-loving plants
which will last all season (Vitax Q4 for
trees and shrubs, for example).

There are plenty of dwarf rhododendrons to choose from. I like *R.
yakushimanum* because, apart from its pale
pink flowers in spring, it has attractive silvery grey new foliage and a good, domed
shape which make it interesting all year
round. Even the undersides of the leaves
are worth noticing, as, like many other rhododendrons, they are covered in a felty
brown 'indumentum'. There are many
*yakushimanum* hybrids but to me the
species is hard to beat.

## PLANTS

1 One spotted laurel (*Aucuba japonica* 'Variegata').
2 One *Pittosporum tenuifolium* 'Tom Thumb'.
3 Two ivies (*Hedera helix* 'Königers Auslese').
4 Three *Hyacinth* 'White Pearl'.
5 Fifteen crocus 'Pickwick'.
6 Two *Libertia peregrinans*.

**CONTAINER** Swag and Acanthus pot from Wichford Pottery measuring 15½ inches (39.5 cm) high and 22 inches (56 cm) diameter.

**POSITION** Suitable for any position, including north-facing, but not deep

This accommodating planting should succeed almost anywhere, including those difficult, often grimy basement areas of city terraces. *Aucuba japonica* 'Variegata' is dominant, and a tougher plant it would be difficult to find. If you can live with its ordinariness, it will provide dependable evergreen all year round.

With pot-raised plants, one can plant up at any time of the year, although autumn is preferable. Crock the base well with broken clay pots or expanded clay pebbles and use a John Innes No. 3 compost with added peat and grit or a mixture of equal amounts of John Innes No. 2 and a peat-based compost. Add the bulbs at the correct height while filling in around the roots of the other plants. Plant crocus 2 to 3 inches (5 to 7.5 cm) deep and hyacinths 4 to 5 inches (10 to 13 cm) deep. Leave a good margin at the top for watering, which should be checked regularly, even in winter. Give a top-dressing of slow-release fertiliser every spring.

As well as the usual spotted laurel, there are some other handsome, if not always subtle, forms to choose from. The brightest is 'Picturata', its leaves splashed with gold in wide central markings. Leaves of 'Crotonifolia' look as though the usual spots have grown out of control into a hectic mottling. If required, prune stray stems back hard in April. Pittosporums may succumb to hard frosts or freezing wind damage but are lovely foliage plants. One of the toughest is *P. tenuifolium* 'Tom Thumb' which matures into a pudding basin-shaped evergreen shrub about 3 feet (91 cm) high and wide. Young foliage is bright green in spring and summer but matures into a reddish bronze in winter. This winter colouring as well as its robust constitution make it a useful plant for containers.

Libertia is a perennial in the iris family which prefers a sheltered spot. White flowers are produced in summer but the plant is mainly grown for its orange-coloured foliage. Eventually the plants will form clumps which can be divided in spring. This could be substituted by ophiopogon, liriope or an evergreen hardy fern like *Polystichum setiferum*.

The choice of spring bulbs can be a personal one with virtually any but the tallest kinds of daffodil and tulip being suitable. Should you be gardening in a very small space and need more summer colour, grow the bulbs in pots or buy them in bud. Plunge these into the container so that after flowering they can be easily removed. Replace with a few pots of summer bedding plants in late May or early June.

## PLANTS

1 One blueberry (*Vaccinium corymbosum* 'Bluetta').
2 Five cranberry (*Vaccinium macrocarpon* 'Early Black').

**CONTAINER** Wooden barrel from Knollys Road Garden Centre measuring 14 inches high (35.5 cm) and 15 inches (38 cm) diameter.

**POSITION** Full sun.

It is exciting to find a plant ideal for a container which is both attractive and fruitful, especially if it is difficult to grow in ordinary garden soil. This is true of highbush blueberries, North American plants which need a very acid soil of pH 4.5 to 5.2 to do well. Blueberry flowers are rather like those of *Pieris*, appearing from March to May and smelling like cowslips. These give way to berries up to ¾ inch (2 cm) across, of superb flavour and texture and you can reckon on enough for five large blueberry pies from one established bush. After the berries have been cropped, autumn colour is bright red and even in winter the red stems are attractive.

Planting of pot-grown plants can be at any time but spring is ideal. Make sure the container has good drainage holes, then crock the base with large expanded clay pebbles, broken pots or bricks. Use an ericaceous plant compost (specially for-mulated for acid-loving plants). Plant the blueberry with perhaps some cranberries round the edge as they like the same con-ditions. Blueberries crop better if two varieties are grown for cross-pollination. A sunny position will ensure that this year's growth is ripened for next year's fruiting. Being acid-lovers, these plants dislike hard tap water and will need rain water. If you are forced to use tap water, add a half-strength liquid feed for acid-loving plants to each watering. Begin regular feeding with a high-potash fertiliser weekly from flowering until when the berries begin to ripen.

No pruning is necessary for the first three years. After this, every March, simply cut out the oldest stems either back to the base or to a healthy, productive stem to encourage strong, new growth. Fruit is produced at the ends of previous years' growths, which then produce side shoots for next year's crop.

Virtually any type of fruit can be grown in a container. Apples, pears, plums and cherries can be grown as dwarf pyramids. Apricots and peaches make successful pot specimens as do gooseberries. (See p. 20 for figs.)

### Stockist

Blueberries and cranberries from James Trehane and Sons Ltd, Stapehill Road, Hampreston, Nr Wimborne, Dorset BH21 7NE.

## PLANTS

1 Common or roof houseleek (red form of *Sempervivum tectorum*).
2 Cobweb houseleek (*Sempervivum arachnoideum*).

**CONTAINER** Terracotta strawberry pot from Wetheriggs Country Pottery measuring 18½ inches (47 cm) high and 15¾ inches (40 cm) diameter.

**POSITION** Full sun.

The intended use for strawberry pots is obvious but I find the smaller ones make ideal containers for succulent plants like these pretty sempervivums. Most are hardy, do not die down in winter and for their size have quite large flower spikes. My favourite is the cobweb houseleek which looks as though a colony of spiders has been hard at work spinning webs over the tightly packed rosettes of leaves. It has its origins in the mountains of Europe, particularly the Pyrenees, and produces tall stems of rose-red flowers in June and July. This red form of *S. tectorum*, another European species, makes a pleasant contrast to the silveriness of *S. arachnoideum*.

Planting time is either in September or April. Place a layer of broken clay pots or expanded clay pebbles in the base before filling the container with a John Innes No. 2 compost with added grit or coarse sand. Pot the plants firmly into the holes as you fill the container and they will soon spread out, new rosettes overflowing most attractively. A mass of plants in the top looks particularly good with a dressing of stone chippings. This holds the new plants firm, stops water from splashing compost up on to the plants, and prevents the rosettes from rotting. Do take care, though, that all the plants receive enough moisture by carefully watering into the holes as well as on top.

As houseleeks are hardy, the container can be maintained outside for as long as it remains attractive. After a while, the plants will run out of space and become congested. Either in September or April, divide the clumps and add fresh compost. As offsets are readily produced, there will be plenty of rosettes with roots attached to use elsewhere or give to friends.

There is a vast range of different sempervivums and their close relatives, jovibarbas to choose form (*see below for stockist*). Having succeeded with these, you might like to try another container with similar but different plants, say, sedums or stonecrops. Read up on the plants before you buy, as not all of them are hardy and some would be too large for this container. *Sedum obtusatum* is a low grower with plump, succulent leaves turning a good bronze-red in summer. *Sedum spathulifolium* from the western United States is widely available and even lower growing, with silver and bronze leaves. I like *S.s.* 'Cape Blanco', a North American of low, mat-like growth and silvery appearance. For taller-growing kinds to plant in the top, go for *S. sieboldii* from Japan or *S. kamschaticum* and its varieties from northeast Asia. Displays could be augmented with some of the attractive echeverias, but remove them for the winter as they are tender.

### Stockist

Alan C. Smith, 127 Leaves Green Road, Keston, Kent BR2 6DG.

**PLANTS**

1 One variegated New Zealand flax
   (*Phormium tenax* 'Variegatum').
2 Two *Artemisia absinthium* 'Lambrook
   Silver'.
3 One *Heuchera* 'Palace Purple'.
4 One rose 'Red Bells'.
5 One rose 'Nozomi'.
6 Two trailing crinkly-leaved ivy.
7 One rose 'Smarty'.

**CONTAINER** Square Hardwood Tub in
natural wood from Pamal measuring 26
inches (66 cm).

**POSITION** Full sun or sun for most of the
day.

This is a container deserving a prominent
position where the contrasting form of the
plants, the exciting colour combinations of
silver, purple and pink, as well as the
beauty of the ground-cover roses, can be
admired. This container looks best slotted
into a corner with the phormium at the
back and a profusion of rose 'Nozomi' and
ivy pouring over the front corner.

As these plants are hardy, planting
could take place at virtually any time provided all the plants arrived in containers.
However, to get the roses you want, you
may have to order them from specialists to
be sent through the post bare-rooted
between autumn and spring. Place a layer
of broken crocks or bricks in the bottom for
good drainage, then use a mixture of John
Innes No. 2 with added peat and grit or
equal parts of John Innes No. 2 and a peat-
based compost. Keep well watered
throughout summer and liquid-feed
monthly with a well-balanced fertiliser.

For a container this size, the tall sword-
like foliage of the New Zealand flax is in
proportion, and lends an exotic, subtropical feel. I find the association of these three
similar but different roses pleasant.
'Nozomi', bred in Japan, is a miniature with
good creeping habit, its sprays of small
pearly-pink flowers appearing in midsummer. 'Red Bells' has darker, crimson-red,
double, rosette-shaped flowers in July and
August and was bred in Denmark. To
complete the trio is 'Smarty', an English-
bred rose with single, soft-pink flowers.
Repeat flowering will ensure a continuation of rose blooms all summer.

The container can remain planted up to
continue giving pleasure for a further summer season as the plants are hardy and
none are going to die down leaving bare
spaces. Both artemisia and heuchera retain
their foliage. The roses are likely to create
problems towards the end of the season by
sending out long, trailing stems. By pruning these back, it is possible to keep them
within bounds for perhaps one more season, then they could be lifted and used in
the garden. Patio roses would make a
longer-lasting choice. There are many
varieties to choose from, varying from 1 to
2 feet (30 to 60 cm) in height. If you want
the container to carry on for a long period,
these roses have the advantage of remaining small but will not have the attractive,
draping habit of the ground coverers. In
time, the New Zealand flax will become
too large and will need to be lifted out one
spring, divided and a portion replaced.
Heuchera can also simply be divided in
spring or autumn. Artemisia can be pruned
back in spring if it grows too tall.

**PLANT**
One fig 'White Adriatic'.

**CONTAINER** Imitation bronze container from Andrew Crace Designs measuring 20 inches (51 cm) high and 16½ inches (42 cm) diameter.

**POSITION** Sheltered and in full sun.

**N**atives of Afghanistan and Persia, figs were introduced into Britain by the Romans. This simulated bronze container is just right to set off the wonderfully architectural foliage. This particular variety has large round fruit with a pale green skin turning almost white when ripe. The flavour is rich and sweet and the flesh inside a strong strawberry colour. There are many varieties available (see stockists below) of which 'Brown Turkey' is by far the most common and will also perform well in a pot.

Although a container-grown plant can be potted up at any time, March is the best month. Use John Innes No. 3 potting compost with added peat and grit. Drainage is important, so if the container has only one hole I would place some crocks over it to prevent clogging. Ideally it should be raised just above the ground to allow free drainage. Water well during summer and feed weekly with a high-potash liquid fertiliser from May until the end of summer.

Root restriction is necessary for successful fruit production but the container will take care of this. Every spring, remove some compost from the top of the pot and top-dress with some fresh John Innes No. 3. A warm, sheltered, bright position is important.

The tiny embryo figs produced towards the end of the season, and which stay on the plant throughout winter, are those that will ripen during the following year to be cropped in August and September. Fruits which develop in spring should be removed in order to channel the energy into those that will ripen. Stop shoots to four or five leaves in June to encourage the production of more sturdy fruit-bearing shoots. In March, cut out damaged or congested stems. Keep a look out for good young stems which can be encouraged up from the base to replace older, less productive ones, in due course.

Unless the fig is sheltered or grown in the warmer parts of the country, some winter protection is needed – ideally bringing the fig indoors into a porch, greenhouse or even a shed. Left outside, straw or dry bracken can be wrapped around all the shoots after the leaves have fallen. This is easier when the fig is tied in to a wall. However, with another pair of helping hands it should be possible to tie the stems loosely together and then work the dry bracken around them, binding it with string as you go.

### Stockists

Reads Nursery, Hales Hall, Loddon, Norfolk NR4 6QW (National Collection holders).

J. Tweedie Fruit Trees, 504 Denby Dale Road West, Calder Grove, Wakefield, Yorkshire WF4 3DB.

Deacon's Nursery, Godshill, Isle of Wight PO38 3HW.

North Hill Nurseries, Scotts Grove Road, Chobham, Surrey GU24 8DW.

## PLANTS

1 Three bulbs of *Lilium regale.*
2 One *Heuchera micrantha* 'Palace Purple'.
3 One *Pieris japonica* 'Little Heath'.
4 Three *Houttuynia cordata* 'Chameleon'.
5 One *Hedera helix* 'Sagittifolia'.
6 One curly-leaved ivy.
7 One *Geranium renardii.*
8 One sun spurge (*Euphorbia cyparissias*).

**CONTAINER** Simulated bronze tub from Andrew Crace Designs measuring 20 inches (51 cm) high and 16½ inches (42 cm) diameter.

**POSITION** Sun or semi-shade.

This stately container takes on a cool, classic look planted with contrasting foliage plants. To maintain all-year-round interest, some of the plants should be kept in their pots which are plunged into the container so they can be replaced as they stop flowering. One might start off with a pot of tall wallflowers, followed by the lilies. Later, a pot of spring-planted *Nerine bowdenii* will add autumn colour.

All the plants are hardy but May is the best time for planting, as by this time the more obvious shapes and sizes of the plants will make positioning easier. Place a good layer of broken pots or expanded clay pebbles in the base before filling in with John Innes No. 2 compost with added peat and sharp sand or equal amounts of John Innes No. 2 and a peat-based compost. Arrange the plants for a good balance of foliage and shape, keeping the wallflowers/lilies/nerine, houttuynia and euphorbia in their pots. Keep moist during summer and liquid-feed monthly with a well-balanced fertiliser.

Heuchera is a striking plant for container arrangements, with its purple leaves and haze of tiny white flowers in summer. When the clump outgrows the container it is an easy matter to lift in spring or autumn, divide and replant. Use the remainder to start off a patch of weed-smothering ground cover which will do well in semi-shade. Another good ground coverer is *Geranium renardii*, a hardy border geranium with exquisite sage-green leaves and purple-veined white flowers in early summer. Variegated interest is provided by *Houttuynia cordata* 'Chameleon', with its leaves of pink, green and yellow. I would restrict it to a pot to prevent its spreading too rapidly. *Euphorbia cyparissias* is also best confined to a pot. Its foliage creates a pool of bright, feathery green topped by characteristic euphorbia flowers. Always wear gloves to handle euphorbias as their sap is poisonous and can cause a nasty rash.

Ivies tumble over the edge and there are so many to choose from that these are only two suggestions. The only shrub in the arrangement is *Pieris* 'Little Heath', a variegated, dwarf version of the larger kinds grown for their bright-red new shoots.

In autumn, remove plants that have died down and replace with winter/spring flowering plants, bulbs or evergreens.

### Stockist

Ivies from Fibrex Nurseries Ltd, Honeybourne Road, Pebworth, Nr Stratford-on-Avon, CV37 8XT.

## PLANTS

1 One Himalayan jasmine (*Jasminum humile* 'Revolutum').
2 Three *Ophiopogon planiscapus nigrescens*.
3 Six golden ling (golden/red forms of *Calluna vulgaris*).

**CONTAINER** Basket Flowerpot from Wichford Pottery measuring 7½ inches (19 cm) high and 20 inches (51 cm) diameter.

**POSITION** Sheltered and in good light.

This is an unusual combination planted as much for its contrasting foliage colour and shape as for flower colour. Himalayan jasmine is one of the least grown of the group and though it bears a passing colour resemblance to the more common but hardier and untidier winter jasmine (*J. nudiflorum*) it is truly evergreen in nature. Flowers, appearing in July and August, are fragrant.

Plant the container in spring, so that the jasmine has a chance of becoming established before it flowers. Crock, or place a layer of expanded clay pebbles over the bottom to assist the passage of water. Using an ericaceous plant compost which will suit the acid-loving calluna, fill in around the plants, leaving a good gap at the top to allow for watering. Keep moist throughout summer, using soft rain water when possible and liquid-feed at the beginning of July and August. If you decide to keep the container going for another season, a top-dressing of slow-release fertiliser suitable for acid-loving plants sprinkled over the surface of the compost in spring should prove adequate.

The jasmine is not self-clinging and will need to be supported by a bamboo cane.

As the jasmine is not in flower for long it is essential to have some exciting foliage, admirably provided by ophiopogon, one of my favourite container plants. This always looks interesting, rather like a sinister, hardy black spider plant. However, simply planting it straight into the garden does not do it justice, as its leaves dangle dismally in the soil and become lost against the dark background. Draping over the sides of a container it is at its most effective. A slow grower, the clump gradually enlarges, sending up fresh shoots a small way from the plant. Golden ling provides good foliage contrast. Any coloured-leaved variety of erica or calluna will do just as well. I like *C.v.* 'Robert Chapman' and *C.v.* 'Wickwar Flame' for their orange-yellow foliage which turns bright red in winter. Naturally, these will become woody and taller with age; simply clip them back hard after flowering, or in spring to ensure a new flush of foliage.

The evergreen, hardy nature of the plants means that the container should work for a long period, providing all-year-round interest. The jasmine will not require regular pruning, but in time would benefit from a general sort-out each spring, just cutting out weak or winter-damaged stems. For added winter interest there is no reason why a few winter-flowering pansies should not be fitted between the roots of the ling. Small, closely planted groups of crocus bulbs might be another addition for spring but remove both after flowering, when their foliage becomes a nuisance.

**PLANT**
One strawberry tree (*Arbutus unedo*).

**CONTAINER** Wooden half-barrel measuring 13½ inches (34 cm) high and 25 inches (63.5 cm) diameter. Make sure there are adequate drainage holes drilled in the base.

**POSITION** Sunny position preferred.

Sometimes just one beautiful specimen shrub in a container is effective on its own without the distraction of other plants. *Arbutus unedo* has a lot to offer as its white or pinkish bell-shaped flowers are produced from October to December, starting just as those from the previous year are turning into bright, orange-red berries. These are edible but although they resemble round strawberries, they are bland and full of gritty seeds. Natives of the Mediterranean region and south-west Ireland, particularly the lakes of Killarney, plants will grow into trees of 15 to 30 (4.5 to 9 m) feet high in the wild. Restricted to a container, however, they should remain within bounds.

Despite being members of the family *Ericaceae*, the strawberry trees *A. unedo*, *A. andrachne* and *A.* × *andrachnoides* are lime tolerant. My own specimen thrives in a mixture of sandy loam from the garden mixed three parts to one with peat-based compost. A spring-top dressing of a slow-release fertiliser like Vitax Q4 for trees and shrubs is sufficient feed for the rest of the year. Place a layer of expanded clay pebbles on the compost surface as they look attractive and keep moisture in and weeds out.

One might suspect, from studying their countries of origin, a preference for milder climates than our own. However, the size and age of specimens in Britain must mean that plants have survived freezing cold temperatures. In cold, exposed parts, I would place the container in a sheltered place and hope for the best.

### Alternative specimen evergreens

I like *Rhamnus alaternus* 'Argenteo variegata' for its small leaves edged with silvery white. A young, wispy plant is best pruned back by half on all its stems in spring, which will encourage a bushy habit. Like arbutus it would benefit from a sheltered position in the colder parts of the country. *Pittosporum tenuifolium* and myrtle (*Myrtus communis*) are even more tender but so attractive. Fix castors on to the base of the wooden barrel before planting and you can wheel them into some shelter for the winter.

There are, of course, tougher evergreens which would not need cosseting. Small-growing rhododendron varieties will need a compost for acid-loving plants as will the excellent Pieris 'Forest Flame' grown as much for its bright red new shoots as its white bell-shaped flowers. *Aucuba japonica*, the spotted laurel, and its bright, showy varieties are very tough. The hollies are excellent, particularly *Ilex aquifolium* 'Ferox Argentea', perhaps better known as the variegated hedgehog holly. Mahonia and box will stand up well to the weather and some of the taller, more graceful cotoneasters are suitable. Look for those grafted as standards so that the top growth weeps attractively. Standard forms of *Cotoneaster* 'Hybridus Pendulus' and *C. dammeri* 'Coral Beauty' are good examples.

## PLANTS

1 One Japanese maple (*Acer palmatum dissectum*).
2 Seven *Ophiopogon planiscapus nigrescens*.

**CONTAINER** Wooden half-barrel measuring 13½ inches (34 cm) high and 25 inches (63.5 cm) diameter.

**POSITION** Will do well in sun or semi-shade.

There are some good deciduous trees and shrubs which make excellent container plants. *Acer palmatum dissectum* is my favourite. A small tree, it has delightful new lime-green foliage in spring and luminous orange-red autumn colour. Although effective on its own, a good underplanting is provided by the ophiopogon, a hardy perennial resembling a black spider plant, best set off by a top-dressing of expanded clay pebbles. Short spikes of small lilac flowers are produced in summer. A scattering of early-spring-flowering crocus would be an added bonus.

The best times for planting are between autumn and early spring, while the acer is dormant. A compost of John Innes No. 2 with added peat and grit or a mixture of equal amounts of John Innes No. 2 and a peat-based compost would be ideal. Keep well watered in summer and give an annual spring top-dressing of slow-release fertiliser.

The only drawback with this type of acer is that they are very expensive to buy as large specimens. For a longer-term project, it might be worth sowing seed of *Acer palmatum*, which will give a mixture of delightful small trees. Plants grow on surprisingly quickly, so that before long a decision can be made as to which might make the best container specimens.

Other Japanese maples for containers include the purple-leaved form, *A.p.* 'Dissectum Atropurpureum', the taller *A.p.* 'Atropurpureum' and *A.p.* 'Osakazuki'. Many other deciduous trees and shrubs will give a good account of themselves. Hydrangea will prefer a shady spot. *Aralia elata* 'Aureo variegata' is ugly in winter but spectacular in summer with arching stems of variegated leaflets. Known as the Japanese angelica tree, it likes sun or partial shade. *Cedrela sinensis* 'Flamingo' has beautiful pink new leaves in spring, is graceful in summer and has good autumn colour.

### Stockists

Acer seed from Chilterns Seeds, Bortree Stile, Ulverston, Cumbria LA12 7PB. *Cedrela sinensis* 'Flamingo' from Burncoose and Southdown Nurseries, Gwennap, Redruth, Cornwall TR16 6BJ.

**PLANTS**

1 One mezereon (*Daphne mezereum*).
2 Ten hardy winter-flowering cyclamen (*Cyclamen coum roseum*).

**CONTAINER** Terracotta from Rockinghams Garden Centre measuring 13 inches (33 cm) high and 12½ inches (32 cm) diameter.

**POSITION** A slightly sheltered, semi-shady spot would be ideal.

WARNING
Berries of *D. mezereum* are very poisonous.

Although deciduous, this small shrub bears a profusion of fragrant, bright pinkish-purple flowers from February to April on leafless stems, so it is not bare for long. Red fruits follow the flowers and the greenish-grey foliage provides some attraction for the summer. There is also a white-flowered form. However, the first surprise with this container will be the brave appearance of hardy cyclamen flowers in December.

Plant this container at any time during winter when the daphne should be more available in garden centres and pots of winter-flowering cyclamen might also be around. To be sure of obtaining the cyclamen you want, it may be best to order in advance from a specialist. To suit both plants, I would use two parts of John Innes No. 2 compost mixed with one part each of sharp sand or grit and leaf mould. Be sure to crock the bottom of the container to ensure good drainage. Should you intend moving corms from the garden, do this in late summer or early autumn. Plant just under the surface of the compost. Keep the compost moist at all times but not saturated and apply a slow-release fertiliser from the second spring onwards, which will last all season. Be vigilant, in spring, for signs of aphids on the new leaves. These must be controlled at once or foliage will be distorted for the rest of the summer. Use a spray designed to kill only aphids so that any ladybirds, ladybird larvae or other aphid predators are not harmed.

For an evergreen daphne rather than the *D. mezereum* photographed, I strongly recommend *Daphne odora* 'Aureo-marginata'. Leaves have narrow, creamy-coloured margins and on a compact, bushy shrub are attractive all year. Between January and April the flowers open and release their strong, delightful fragrance. Although the shrub is hardy it also makes an excellent specimen for an unheated porch.

Hardy cyclamen are easy to grow from seed, particularly when ripe. This is not always easy to obtain. If you are forced to use dry seed, allow it to soak in water until it has plumped up. Sow onto the surface of one part John Innes No. 3 mixed with one part of coarse sand and one of moss peat. Cover with a thin layer of grit, leave outside and germination will take place at the same time as plants naturally come into growth. When pricking out, give seedlings plenty of room and they will quickly grow into large plants.

## PLANTS

1 One *Skimmia japonica* 'Rubella'.
2 Five pots or 15 bulbs of *Scilla mischtschenkoana*.
3 Five pink winter-flowering heathers (*Erica carnea* 'Springwood White').

**CONTAINER** Thai glazed pot measuring 16 inches (40 cm) high and 18 inches (46 cm) in diameter.

**POSITION** Sun or semi-shade. A north-facing position would be suitable.

For a prominent position by the front door of a house with a formal approach, a container of smart, structural plants is particularly appropriate. This simple arrangement of skimmia with winter-flowering heathers and bulbs fits the bill. The evergreen shape will not vary throughout the year, then there are the tightly packed red buds of the skimmia to look forward to in winter. These stay tightly shut, then magically open to small white flowers in spring.

I would favour an autumn planting. Crock the bottom of the container with broken clay pots or expanded clay pebbles. For the benefit of the skimmia, which prefers a slightly acid soil, use a compost for acid-loving plants. The scilla bulbs should be planted 2 inches (5 cm) deep. Check regularly for watering, even in winter. Top-dress with a slow-release fertiliser in spring which should then last for the whole growing season. Once the heathers have finished flowering they should be trimmed back hard to encourage new growth and avoid long, straggly plants.

This arrangement of plants should remain fresh and interesting for some years. Any small spring-flowering bulbs can be used to add colour. Narcissus, crocus, puschkinias, snowdrops, chionodoxa or the deeper blue *Scilla sibirica* would be ideal. Were they not planted as bulbs in the autumn, there is another chance to add them in early spring. Pots of bulbs just coming into growth usually begin appearing in garden centres and markets from about the end of January. These should only just be showing above the compost. Providing the container does not dry out during winter when their roots are growing and they have the opportunity to 'refuel' by staying in leaf after flowering until naturally dying down for the summer, they should come up every year.

Skimmias are small shrubs ideal for containers. *S. japonica* 'Rubella' is a male variety, which means that although blessed with attractive flowers, it will never produce those pretty red fruits some other skimmias are grown for. To be sure of these it is necessary to plant a female variety in the container and have a male nearby for pollination. When male flowers are full of pollen, remove one and brush it over the female flowers to ensure a good set. *S. reevesiana* 'Robert Fortune' does not need a pollinator as both male and female flowers open on the same plant.

Another small evergreen, grown as much for its domed shape and long, oval leaves as flower or fruit is *Viburnum davidii*. This, too, is shade tolerant. Small white flowers appear in June and after pollination are followed by turquoise fruits in September. Again, female plants will only bear fruit if a male plant is nearby.

## PLANTS

1 One stinking hellebore (*Helleborus foetidus*).
2 Nine bulbs of *Scilla mischtschenkoana*.
3 One variegated ivy (*Hedera helix* 'Glacier').
4 One clump of *Arum italicum marmoratum*.

**CONTAINER** Terracotta wall container measuring 8½ inches (21.5 cm) high and 14 inches (35.5 cm) across the front of the top.

**POSITION** Ideal for a shady place, this container would suit a north-facing wall.

W all containers are a pretty alternative to hanging baskets and window boxes, useful where there is no depth of window ledge or space for baskets. Used singly or *en masse*, they brighten up a plain expanse of wall or add interest beside doors. Using the ideas put forward for hanging baskets, no end of plant combinations are possible. This arrangement is particularly useful as it will tolerate sun or shade.

The ideal planting time is autumn, so that scilla bulbs can be added around the other plants. Alternatively, pots of small bulbs in growth can be obtained from garden centres and planted in amongst the other plants in February. Use John Innes No. 2 with added peat and grit or equal amounts of John Innes No. 2 and a peat-based compost. Leave a margin at the top for watering, which must become a matter of routine as the pot is likely to be in the rain shadow of the building. A sprinkling of slow-release fertiliser in spring should be adequate for the rest of the season. Alternatively, give monthly liquid feeds with a balanced fertiliser from May to September.

Despite its rather unfortunate name, the stinking hellebore will give bold, evergreen foliage shape at the back of the arrangement. Pale buds rise up during winter into a cluster of nodding, greenish, cup-shaped flowers with red rims in early spring. An over-large clump can easily be divided or replaced.

*Arum italicum marmoratum* is an invaluable winter foliage plant, producing its marbled leaves in the autumn and dying down in the summer. I keep a good clump in the garden for continual use in winter flower arrangements and to lift for winter containers. A mature clump will flower in late spring, followed by a stalk of bright red poisonous berries. Any kind of small-leaved ivy will look good trailing over the edge of the pot, as well as the blue-flowered lesser periwinkle (*Vinca minor*). Any small, early spring-flowering bulbs would be suitable – small crocus, *Scilla sibirica*, puschkinia or chionodoxa. Providing the compost is not allowed to dry out in winter, they should appear every spring.

## PLANTS

1 Seven pink tulips (*Tulipa* 'Primavera').
2 Nine white tulips (*Tulipa* 'Inzell').
3 Eight blue winter- and spring-flowering pansies.

**CONTAINER** Blue glazed pot from Rockinghams Garden Centre measuring 10½ inches (26.5 cm) high and 14½ inches (37 cm) diameter.

**POSITION** Sun for most of the day.

Successful container planting is dependent on aesthetic as well as practical considerations. Plants should associate well together, complementing each others' shape and colouring. Thought must also be given to the matching of plants with the container. The wrong plants will not only look out of scale but might suffer culturally – small plants being prone to waterlogging in a large container, and a huge plant becoming dry and cramped in a small container. Sometimes it is satisfying to be able to pick up a colour from the container and echo it in the planting. Here, the faint blue tinge in the glaze of the pot is emphasised by the stronger blue of the pansies.

Plant in the autumn, preferably November. Crock the base well, then use John Innes No. 2 with added peat and grit or a mixture of equal amounts of John Innes No. 2 and a peat-based compost. Stop filling when 6 inches (15 cm) from the top. Arrange the tulip bulbs on the compost, beginning with 'Primavera' in the centre, then 'Inzell' on the outside.

The number of bulbs used will vary from container to container. As long as they are not touching each other or the sides, the spacing is correct. Fill in around the bulbs with compost, planting a circle of pansies at the edge so that the compost stops an inch below the top to allow for watering. Check for watering regularly throughout autumn, winter and spring. Once the tulips have finished flowering they can be lifted out and planted in the garden to make way for summer bedding.

This is just one combination of tulips. Great fun can be had planning which varieties to grow together, contrasting colours and matching heights and flowering times. Another favourite combination would be double late varieties 'Mount Tacoma' and 'Angelique', white and pink respectively. Myosotis (forget-me-nots) associate well with tulips, making a froth of blue under the rising flower stalks. Bellis make a bolder statement with their white, red or pink daisy flowers. To extend the flowering season of the bulbs, plant the tulips a little deeper, sprinkle compost on top, then add a layer of daffodils before filling in and adding the other plants. The daffodils will appear first, then the tulips.

There are plenty of winter and spring bedding plants in the garden centres in autumn but they are easy to raise from seed. Conveniently, these are sown after the mad rush of germinating, pricking out, hardening off and planting out the summer bedding. Sowings made in May and June will give good results. One advantage lies in being able to choose which variety to grow. Universal pansy 'True Blue' or even better pansy 'Joker Light Blue' (Suttons Seeds) would look particularly good.

## PLANTS

1 One Christmas box (*Sarcococca ruscifolia*).
2 Six pots or 18 bulbs of yellow bulbous reticulata iris (*Iris danfordiae*).
3 One plain green-leaved thyme.
4 One golden thyme.
5 One silver thyme.
6 Three *Primula gracilipes.*
7 One *Saxifraga* × *urbium* 'Variegata'.
8 One *Hebe pimeleoides* 'Quicksilver'.
9 Seven bulbs of *Narcissus* 'Topolino'.
10 One *Euphorbia amygdaloides robbiae*.
11 Five corms of *Crocus* 'Remembrance'.

**CONTAINERS**  A. Terracotta pot from Rockinghams Garden Centre measuring 12½ inches (32 cm) high and 13 inches (33 cm) diameter.
B. Terracotta half pot from Wichford Pottery measuring 8 inches (20 cm) high and 14 inches (35.5 cm) in diameter.
C. Terracotta pot from Bryan's Garden Centre measuring 13 inches (33 cm) high and 11 inches (28 cm) diameter.

**POSITION**  Sun or semi-shade. This group would suit a north-facing position.

**W**here there are no garden borders and the only way to introduce plants is to use containers, a group of different pots, bowls, urns or tubs will create greater impact. Choose plants which like the same conditions, although, as we have done here, it is possible to cheat slightly.

Planting is best carried out in the autumn. However, pots of bulbs can be bought in flower from garden centres in early spring. Once the plants are in place, there is no reason why most of them can-not remain in the containers for several years. Crock the base of each container well. Use John Innes compost No. 2 with added peat and grit or a mixture of equal amounts of John Innes No. 2 and a peat-based compost. Check regularly for watering throughout the year. A sprinkling of slow-release fertiliser in spring should prove adequate feeding for the whole growing season. Alternatively, liquid-feed monthly from May to September.

When planting a group, using the same plant or colour in two or more of the containers provides some continuity. Here, pretty *Iris danfordiae* will link two pots together when its 4-inch (10-cm) high yellow flowers open in early spring. The season of interest is long, with the low evergreen sarcococca producing small white, scented flowers during winter, followed by red berries. Dwarf daffodil 'Topolino' will open its creamy white and pale lemon flowers in March followed by the exquisite late-spring flowers of *Primula gracilipes*. The silvery foliage of the hebe and strong variegated effect of the saxifrage will be of interest all year round.

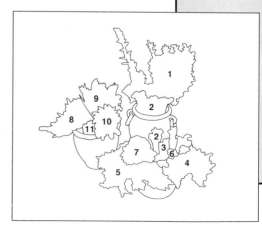

## PLANTS

1 Fifteen bulbs of *Narcissus* 'Las Vegas'.
2 Three red winter/spring-flowering pansies.
3 Three gold winter/spring-flowering pansies.

**CONTAINER** Pale terracotta pot from Andrew Crace Designs measuring 20 inches (51 cm) high and 18 inches (46 cm) diameter.

**POSITION** Full sun will be appreciated.

**R**ather than allowing attractive containers to lie idle and empty in winter, fill them with a simple mixture of whichever spring-flowering plants and bulbs catch your eye. There need be no searching high and low for unusual specimens or spending a fortune on shrubs and herbaceous plants. This is just one possible combination out of many, using daffodils and richly coloured pansies.

Plant in autumn, crocking the container thoroughly with broken pots or expanded clay pebbles. If the pot was previously occupied by summer bedding, it might be possible to retain some of the old compost and crocks to save money. Otherwise, use John Innes No. 2 compost with added peat and grit or a mixture of equal amounts of John Innes No. 2 and a peat-based compost. Arrange the pansies around the edge and plant the daffodil bulbs so that their tips or 'noses' are buried by about 2 inches (5 cm) of compost. Check regularly for water as, even during winter, containers can dry out to the detriment of the plants. Pansies are often attacked by aphids, so examine regularly and take action before flowers and leaves become distorted.

Another of my favourite combinations would be achieved by substituting the daffodils for rich red and orange coloured wallflowers. These, combined with the gold and red pansies, give a wonderfully warm effect. Wallflowers may look somewhat bedraggled in autumn and winter but begin to pick up as soon as light, then natural warmth, gradually improve. By April and May they should look their best and smell delicious. For a small container or trough the Siberian wallflower (*Cheiranthus × allionii*) is ideal. Shorter plants with warm orange, perfumed flowers, they would associate well with smaller bulbs like crocus or scilla.

To make this planting even more economical, plants could be raised from seed. No extra heat is required as sowing takes place in late spring or early summer. Wallflower seed can be sown directly into drills in the ground. Once the seedlings are large enough to handle, they should be spaced 6 inches (15 cm) apart and grown on until ready to be used in the autumn for garden or container. I prefer to sow pansies into pots during June or July, pricking them out into seed trays. For special plants, they can be moved on again into small pots before being planted into the container.

## PLANTS

1 One thrift (*Armeria juniperifolia*).
2 One houseleek (*Sempervivum tectorum* form).
3 One *Saxifraga paniculata* form.
4 One *Primula marginata* form.
5 One *Erodium × variabile* 'Album'.
6 One *Saxifraga cuneifolia* 'Variegata'.

**CONTAINER** Trough for alpines measuring 18 inches (45 cm) long, 8 inches (20 cm) wide and 7 inches (17 cm) high.

**POSITION** Full sun or sun for most of the day.

For alpine plant lovers unable to find the space for a rock garden, growing a variety of small plants in a stone sink or trough could be the answer. Avoid choosing plants which grow and spread too rapidly. This container is prettily planted with cushion-forming types. A taller plant and one or two of trailing habit would add variation to the theme.

Genuine stone sinks are rare and expensive, so most examples are old white or brown glazed sinks craftily covered with a mixture referred to as 'hypertufa'. This consists of sifted moss peat (two parts), silver sand (one part) and cement (one part) mixed dry, then water added until it can just about be squeezed out. Make sure the old sink is well scrubbed, allow to dry, then coat with a PVA adhesive which will bond the hypertufa to the surface. Cover with a ¾-inch (2-cm) thickness of hypertufa, being sure to go under the base and down into the inside so that no part of the old sink will be visible. There are various tricks to help the hypertufa look natural. Painting liquid fertiliser over the surface will encourage mosses to colonise, while making pock marks and chisel marks simulates the appearance of old stone.

Drainage is essential, so raise the container up off the ground onto low bricks or stones. Crock the base well and use a John Innes No. 2 compost with added grit to hasten the passage of water. When filling in around the plants, allow space for a top dressing of grit, not only to set off the plants but to prevent splashes of water and soil from spoiling their foliage. Water will also be taken quickly away from the crowns of the plants. Before planting, set one or more rocks into the surface so that they resemble natural strata.

Popular choices for height are dwarf junipers, particularly *J. communis* 'Compressa'. *Helichrysum selago* with compact, scale-like leaves and a dwarf willow, *Salix × boydii* are also effective. I have even used alpine aquilegias for summer height and flower. For creeping over the edge, alpine phlox, alyssum and asperula are ideal.

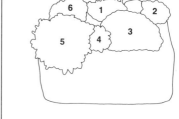

**PLANTS**

**1** One *Artemisia* 'Powis Castle'.
**2** Six *Aptenia cordifolia* 'Variegata'.
**3** Three blue fescue (*Festuca glauca*).

**CONTAINER** Haddenstone Plaited Basket measuring 20 inches (51 cm) long, 15½ inches (39.5 cm) wide and 8½ inches (21.5 cm) high.

**POSITION** Full sun.

An unusual combination of plants, this attractive stone basket is complemented by an emphasis on leaf texture and shape. Reminiscent of the seaside, this container brings to mind succulent plants creeping over cliffs, grasses colonising sand dunes and a shimmering sea.

Plant the basket up in early June when all danger of frost is past. An earlier planting can be made but only with the facility of a greenhouse to protect from late frosts. Artemisia and festuca are hardy plants but the unusual aptenia is frost tender. Crock the container well with broken pots or expanded clay pebbles as good drainge will be essential. Use a John Innes No. 2 compost with added peat and grit or a mixture of equal amounts of John Innes No. 2 and a peat-based compost, again with extra grit to aid the passage of water through the compost. While the container must not be waterlogged, then neither must it be allowed to dry out, so check regularly for watering. Give monthly liquid feeds with a well-balanced fertiliser from planting until late summer.

*Artemisia* 'Powis Castle', with its fine silvery foliage, is a good container plant, providing height and an elegant backdrop for other plants. At the end of the season it could be transferred to a garden border where it will provide a feature all winter, only appearing bedraggled during the worst wet, cold weather. Alternatively, both this and the festuca could remain *in situ* to be livened up with plants for winter and spring interest. An evergreen grass, useful for its spiky, bluish leaves, *Festuca glauca* will make good tufts of growth if left undisturbed. Should the clumps become large and begin to look congested with dead leaves, it may be necessary to lift and divide one spring. Carefully prise the roots and leaves apart, using some to replant in the basket and the rest to form a group in the borders.

Aptenia is a native of South Africa which will quickly knit together to form a mass towards the front of the container. A low-growing, ground-covering succulent, it rarely reaches higher than a couple of inches and needs lots of sun to do well. Take cuttings during summer which, when rooted, can be overwintered in a frost-free greenhouse as small plants for the following year.

Should aptenia be elusive then substitute with a similar succulent like mesembryanthemum, sometimes called Livingstone daisy. These are readily available from garden centres and can be grown from seed. Their foliage may not be as attractive as the variegated aptenia but the larger, daisy-like flowers are a compensation. Either a mixed variety or the yellow-flowered 'Lunette' would be most effective. These really must have sun or their flowers will not open.

## PLANTS

1 One soft shield fern (*Polystichum setiferum*).
2 Two hart's tongue ferns (*Phyllitis scolopendrium*).
3 Two deer fern or hard fern (*Blechnum spicant*).
4 One autumn fern or Japanese shield fern (*Dropteris erythrosora*).
5 One sensitive fern (*Onoclea sensibilis*).

**CONTAINER** Haddonstone Small Alpine Trough measuring 10 inches (25.5 cm) high, 22 inches (56 cm) wide and 32 inches (81 cm) long.

**POSITION** Semi-shade or full shade.

Instead of despairing of a shady corner, look upon it as an excuse to grow a trough of beautiful hardy ferns. They may not flower, but the contrast between the different greens and shapes of their fronds can be more than adequate compensation for a common blaze of colour. There are many hardy ferns from which to choose. Set them off with a rock or two, placed just off centre.

Plant the container in spring, just as the ferns are beginning to grow. A planting mixture consisting of equal amounts of John Innes No. 2, peat, leaf mould and sharp sand should be ideal. Keep moist and give a liquid feed every three weeks during summer.

For good all-year-round interest, the majority of the ferns should be evergreen.

*Polystichum setiferum* and its varieties fit the bill admirably although the fronds do become tatty towards the end of winter. Varieties like *P.s.* 'Divisilobum Densum' have a close, moss-like appearance and are superb in spring as new growth unfurls from the centre of the plant. The hart's tongue fern contrasts well, having tongue-like, shiny, bright green fronds. Both these and *Blechnum spicant*, the hard fern, are native plants, the latter being one of our more common evergreens, with a compact habit making it eminently suitable for the front of the container. *Dryopteris erythrosora* is different in being both deciduous and foreign, originating from Japan and China. Fronds are coppery-pink when young and growth is altogether so attractive that one can forgive it for not being able to maintain this during winter (although it will indoors). *Onoclea sensibilis* is another deciduous foreigner, this time from North America and northern Asia.

As all the ferns are hardy, the arrangement can be left outside indefinitely.

Eventually the ferns will expand and push against each other for space. Divide the old plants in spring, replacing them with smaller crowns. Spores can be gathered and sown. Some polystichums bear tiny plantlets along old fronds, which can be detached and laid on compost in autumn until the babies grow larger and form their own roots.

## PLANTS

1 One yellow flag (*Iris pseudacorus*).
2 One marsh marigold (*Caltha palustris*).
3 One monkey musk (*Mimulus* 'Queen's Prize').
4 Pond weed (*Lagarosiphon major* – used to be known as *Elodea crispa*).
5 One water lily. (This one is *Nymphaea* 'Marliacea Chromatella' but is unsuitable for a container this size. A pygmy water lily must be chosen.)
6 One or two water lettuce (*Pistia stratiotes*).
7 One *Houttuynia cordata* 'Flore Pleno'.
8 One *Darmera peltata* (used to be known as *Peltiphyllum peltatum*).
9 One water forget-me-not (*Myosotis palustris*).

**CONTAINER** Wooden barrel with no drainage holes measuring 13½ inches (34 cm) high and 25 inches (63.5 cm) diameter.

**POSITION** Sun or semi-shade.

To create a simple and cheap pond, a wooden half-barrel sunk into the ground is an excellent idea. There is no need to line the container, provided there are no drainage holes. After all, these barrels usually start out in life as containers for whisky, so they should be capable of holding liquid.

This particular container shows many of the different plants suitable for a pond. In fact there are too many – you will need 2–3 marginal plants, a submerged aquatic for aerating the water and a small water lily. Soon the miniature pond will be teeming with life and of endless fascination to children. I would avoid fish but some frog spawn will soon fill the garden with slug-eating frogs.

Set the pond up in late spring as the plants are coming into growth. Marginal (edge) plants are best potted into special baskets which can be hooked over the edge of the barrel. Garden centres will sell these with some hessian lining and gravel to place on top of the compost. Special compost for aquatics is available, or mix some extra grit and organic slow-release fertiliser (e.g. coarse hoof and horn) with ordinary garden soil. Should the pygmy water lily be bought in a pot, repot into a basket, so that the crown is just above the surface. Place the container in the water on a brick or two, so that the crown is not too deep. This can be lowered gradually as the leaves grow.

Include at least one marginal with variegated foliage. There are many different water irises to choose from but the variegated form of yellow flag is striking. My favourite plant to grow around the outside, perhaps in place of the myosotis, is *Brunnera macrophylla* 'Variegata' with cream-variegated leaves and small blue flowers.

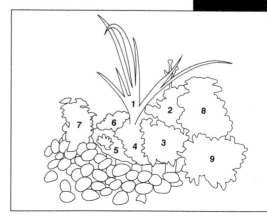

## PLANTS

1 One *Penstemon* 'King George'.
2 Two small pink marguerite
  (*Chrysanthemopsis gayanum* – formerly
  *Argyranthemum mawii*).
3 One thyme (*Thymus longicaulis*).
4 One stork's bill (*Erodium
  glandulosum*).
5 One stonecrop (*Sedum oreganum*).
6 One thrift (*Armeria juniperifolia*).
7 One *Artemisia* 'Powis Castle'.
8 One *Berberis thunbergii* 'Atropurpurea
  Nana'.
9 One yellow sun rose (*Helianthemum*
  'Wisley Primrose').

**CONTAINER** Wichford Oval Pot measuring
8 inches (20 cm) deep and 17 inches
(43 cm) long.

**POSITION** Full sun or sun for most of the
day.

This pleasant combination of yellow and
pink flowers with green, silver and purple
foliage should provide plenty of interest
for the whole summer. The plants used are
not the more conventional bedding plants
but a mixture of small shrubs, rock garden
and herbaceous plants. The chunky terracotta oval bowl is of just the right dimen-
sions to complement the size of the plants.

Planting time would be late spring or
early summer. Although most of these
plants are hardy, the argyranthemum is
frost tender and *Penstemon* 'King George',
although likely to survive a mild winter, is
not reliable. Place a good layer of pebbles
or broken crocks in the base, then use John
Innes No. 2 compost with extra peat and
sharp sand or equal parts of John Innes No.

2 and a peat-based compost. Leave a good
margin for watering. Keep moist during
summer and feed with a well-balanced liquid fertiliser at the beginning of July and
August. Should any of the plants threaten
to swamp their neighbours, be ready to
trim them back within bounds.

The penstemon gives height and interesting shape to the arrangement. There are
many to choose from and most would be
suitable, flowering late into the season.
Although the hardy alpines types are
tough, the more tender ones need frost
protection. I would pot up the penstemon
in the autumn for overwintering or have
taken summer cuttings for a fresh start the
following year. Very much the same
applies to *Chrysanthemopsis gayanum*,
grown for its pretty, warm pink daisy-like
flowers. The rest of the plants should be
hardy enough to be left in the container
through the winter. Easily movable, it
could be stood in a sheltered spot during
long frosty periods when the soil freezes
for such long periods that the plants,
although dormant, begin to suffer for lack
of water.

The gaps left by the absence of the two
tender plants can be filled by spring
bedding like Siberian wallflowers. To
smarten up the container for the following
summer, remove the spring flowerers,
prune back the shrubby plants and tidy the
thrift and sedum. Replace the penstemon
and argyranthemum and begin fortnightly
liquid feeds from late May onwards. As
everything will grow too large and woody
to repeat this for a third season, plan to
propagate or replace most of the plants and
dismantle the container in autumn.

**PLANTS**

1 One *Arabis ferdinandii-coburgii* 'Variegata'.
2 One pink sun rose (*Helianthemum* 'Ben Ledi').
3 *Sedum spathulifolium* 'Cape Blanco'.
4 *Arabis caucasica* 'Variegata'.
5 One brass buttons (*Leptinella pyrethrifolia linearifolia* – formerly *Cotula lineariloba*).
6 *Lewisia* 'Pinkie'.

**CONTAINER** Basket Flowerpot from Wichford Pottery measuring 7½ inches (19 cm) high and 20 inches (51 cm) diameter.

**POSITION** Full sun, or sun for most of the day.

There is such a variety of attractive rock garden plants on sale that the only problem in creating a colourful summer container-ful lies in choosing which to plant. This small terracotta bowl shows a selection of low-growing, sun-loving plants with interesting shape, leaf and flower colour. If unavailable from ordinary garden centres, they can be obtained from specialist nurseries, most of which have a mail-order service.

Buy the plants in spring or early summer. They enjoy a well-drained soil, so crock the base well. A John Innes No. 2 compost with added peat and grit should prove ideal. After planting, top off with a dressing of gravel which will help water pass quickly away from the crowns and leaves of the plants. Keep well watered though not saturated throughout the summer and give a high-potash feed just a couple of times, perhaps at the beginning of July and again at the beginning of August. Should any of the more vigorous plants threaten to take over the smaller ones, cut them back.

Lewisia makes an evergreen clump, producing a profusion of pretty pink flowers in early summer. There is no reason why the plant cannot stay in the container over winter. Small rosettes will form around the main clump which can be removed and potted separately during summer. The vigorous but colourful sun rose can be propagated by cuttings taken in early summer. After flowering, trim back for the winter. In time, the original plant will become large and straggly and should be replaced in spring with a fresh plant raised from a cutting. The silvery-leaved sedum is easy to control. Simply remove what is not required. The succulent leaves make a bright contrast to the darker foliage of the sun rose.

Even variegated arabis are rampant. As with the sedum, carefully dig out parts of the clump at the edges where it threatens to engulf other plants. Leptinella, which produces button-like heads of yellow flowers on thin stalks above a mass of fine, silvery foliage, should not grow too quickly. Leave in the container over winter, but divide the clump in spring, replanting a smaller portion.

**PLANTS**

Five *Lotus maculatus*.

**CONTAINER** Old chimney pot from Bentinck nurseries.

**POSITION** Likes the sun.

Although chimney pots have become popular containers and can cost a lot to buy, it is not always easy to find plants which suit them. There is not much space in the top for a profusion of plants, yet the desired effect is of a cascade of growth over the side. There are two ways of approaching the planting. One is to have a more permanent arrangement which involves standing the chimney pot on a base of some kind in case it should ever need to be moved. Fill the bottom third with pebbles or some other drainage medium, then add compost and plant into the top. I find that because there is so little room in the top, in order to achieve an attractive display for all seasons, it is best to have a variety of clay pots of exactly the right size to sit in the top so that one can easily get a grip on the rims to lift in and out. Small hanging baskets can be used for very trailing plants. Plan a succession of these so that by swapping them around during the year, your pot always looks bright and exciting.

Having decided on the latter regime, you can grow exotic-looking plants which might not be in flower all season. I have chosen *Lotus maculatus*, a relative of the more common coral gem (*L. berthelotii*). The foliage, flower colour and shape make it an ideal complement for the glaze on this particular chimney pot. The fiery red claw-shaped flowers of the coral gem, a native of

Tenerife, would also look good. These plants are at their flowering best around Chelsea Flower Show time (end of May), where they can often be admired in baskets and pots. Fortunately garden centres now stock them more widely. Ideally, one should acquire plants early in the season, plant several into a basket and leave them in greenhouse or porch to grow on. Take care, as they dislike over-watering. I like to see the compost becoming quite dry and the plants almost beginning to wilt before watering again.

Once these are past their glory, they can be removed and replaced by perhaps a spectacular trailing fuchsia. A combination of trailing pelargonium, ivies, petunia and lobelia would look good. Trailing pink or white verbena with the delicate blue flowers and fine foliage of brachycome (Swan River daisy), or the trailing stems and blue-purple saucer flowers of *Convolvulus sabatius* (formerly *C. mauritanicus*) would be another winning combination. Keep well watered and liquid-feed once a week.

Once the summer-flowering display is over, replace with yet another container. Plant dwarf tulips thickly, cover with a small amount of compost, then add a layer of crocus, with some ivy planted in the top. Tulips, ivy and pansies are another good combination. As the tulips can be placed deep in the pot, it should be possible to place the rootballs of the other plants on top. The tulips will still be able to push their way through in the spring. Even during winter a basket or pot in the top of the chimney can still dry out, so check regularly for watering.

**PLANTS**

1 Two hosta.
2 One ornamental onion (*Allium nutans*).
3 Three snakeweed or bistort (*Persicaria bistota* 'Superbum' formerly *Polygonum bistorta* 'Superbum').
4 One *Hypericum olympicum minus*.

**CONTAINER** Terracotta pancheon from Wetheriggs Country Pottery measuring 9 inches (23 cm) high and 24 inches (61 cm) diameter.

**POSITION** Sun or semi-shade.

Although not exactly a riot of colour, this interesting combination of rounded, solid-looking hosta leaves with the wispier flower stems of polygonum, allium and hypericum, is unusual and will tolerate some shade. In a small town garden where lots of containers are used, it is good to have a variety of different kinds of plants and not just the more popular bedding plants.

Planting can take place at virtually any time of the year but I would favour the spring, as the hosta, which forms the main impact, will just be coming into leaf. John Innes No. 2 compost with added peat and grit or a mixture of equal amounts of John Innes No. 2 and peat-based compost will be ideal. Leave a good gap for watering in the top of the container and keep moist. Liquid-feed every month between May and September. Other maintenance will involve removing dead flower stems and leaves. However, do not be in too much of a rush to take off the dead hosta leaves in autumn as, to an extent, they protect the crowns of the plant. As the hosta comes into growth it will pay to keep an eye open for slug attack. If you have pets or worry about birds eating poisoned slugs, ask at the garden centre for one of the products which are only harmful to slugs.

This hosta was chosen because of the solid roundness of its bluish-coloured leaves. However, any large-leaved hosta would look good. *H.* 'Thomas Hogg', *H. fortunei* 'Aurea marginata' and *H. crispula* are all variegated, while *H.* 'Royal Standard' has attractive lime-green leaves. The persicaria will spread itself around the container, sending up its spikes of pink flowers. *Allium nutans* is one of a large group of ornamental plants that belongs in the same family as onions and garlic. This one forms a clump of narrow leaves and produces heads of pink flowers. Cut off any hosta leaves that threaten the clump by shading it from the sun. The hypericum might be an unusual choice, but in a shady spot the usually upright growth will become more spreading and fan out over the front of the container.

As all the plants are hardy, the container can remain planted for as long as the plants associate well together. After the second season, competition for space is likely to be such that they will need to be removed, divided and replaced as smaller clumps.

**PLANTS**

1 One *Abutilon × hybridum* 'Savitzii'.
2 Three ornamental cabbage or kale.

**CONTAINER** Pale terracotta pot from Andrew Crace Designs measuring 18 inches (45 cm) high and 10 inches (25.5 cm) diameter.

**POSITION** Full sun.

This bizarre arrangement of abutilon and cabbage makes a tall, rather amusing container which is bound to catch attention. I find the whole combination pleasant with the pale terracotta contrasting nicely with the dark cabbage leaves and complementing the pale orange of the abutilon flowers.

Planting should take place in spring. The abutilon is tender and should not be stood outside until late May or early June. Crock the base well before adding compost. John Innes No. 2 with added peat and grit or a mixture of equal amounts of John Innes No. 2 and a peat-based compost will be ideal. Water well throughout summer and liquid-feed every three weeks.

*Abutilon* 'Savitzii' and other named varieties will have to be bought in. However, with the help of a greenhouse it should be possible to keep it going from year to year. At the end of the summer, move the plant into a light, frost-free place. A huge unruly plant can be cut back by half in the autumn but leave major pruning until spring, when all the lateral stems can be shortened to within one or two nodes of main stems. Cuttings can be taken of shoot tips during summer or in spring. For those keen to raise their own plants, there are seed mixtures, such as *Abutilon* 'Large Flowered Mixed' from Dobies or Mr Fothergill's, which take about five months to flower from seed. Cabbage can be bought or sown. Although we have used plants with dark ornamental foliage, some are coloured with bright pink, soft pink or cream as well as green. Both these and the abutilon tend to come into their full glory towards late summer.

An alternative variegated abutilon *A. pictum.* 'Thompsonii' has bolder leaves and brighter orange, veined flowers. *A.* 'Ashford Red' is plain-leaved with red bells and *A.* 'Boule de Neige' has white flowers. There are other tender shrubs of similar stature to try. Although one has the bother of over-wintering them, or investing in a new plant each year, they give such good value by flowering all summer long, a feat which some hardy shrubs find hard to emulate.

The unusual *Sphaeralcea umbellata*, a close relative of abutilon, will do well outside during the summer. Normally sold as a greenhouse plant, it might be difficult to find. Datura or angels' trumpets will grow well outdoors during summer. There are many to choose from with flower colours ranging from cream and white, through pale pink to deep pinks and orange-red. They can be pruned really hard and still reliably grow again so that they take up little space in the greenhouse during winter. Seed is freely available. 'Angels' Trumpets Mixed' and *D. suaveolens* (white and perfumed) are available from Thompson and Morgan; *D. metel* (huge double yellow, violet or white flowers) and others from Chiltern Seeds. Take care as all parts of datura are poisonous. Always use gloves when pruning.

## PLANTS

1 One yellow-leaved form of the Mexican orange (*Choisya ternata* 'Sundance').
2 One lemon-scented geranium (*Pelargonium graveolens*).
3 One purple sage (*Salvia officinalis* 'Purpurascens'.
4 One oleander (*Nerium oleander*).

**CONTAINER** Running Leaf Pot from Wichford Pottery measuring 20 inches (51 cm) high and 23 inches (58.5 cm) diameter.

**POSITION** Sunny and sheltered.

WARNING
Oleander is a poisonous plant.

This striking container is planted primarily for the colour and diversity of its foliage.

As the pelargonium and oleander are tender plants, it is an advantage if you have a frost-free greenhouse in which to start the composition off early and give the plants time to knit together before being stood outside at the beginning of June. However, as all specimens can be bought as reasonably good-sized plants, the effect can be virtually instant and a quick assembly in June will work. Most of the plants appreciate a well-drained soil, so be sure to crock the base well. Use a John Innes No. 2 compost with added peat and grit or sharp sand. Alternatively, mix together equal amounts of John Innes No. 2 and a peat-based compost.

The plants will be bright and interesting all summer long. Although flowers are not the priority, they will be a welcome bonus.

If you do not keep picking the tips out of the sage to use in cooking, it will run up into spikes of purple-blue flowers in June and July. The lemon-scented geranium is pleasant to smell as you brush past and will produce small rose-pink flowers with a purple spot on each of the upper petals all summer. Oleander should produce a succession of flowers. We have chosen a strong pink but there are pale pink, white, double-flowered and other varieties to choose from. The performance of all the plants will be enhanced by a sunny, sheltered position. Never allow the container to dry out and liquid-feed monthly.

At summer's end there are several options. With the refuge of a frost-free greenhouse, the container can remain undisturbed for the following year. In spring, apply a slow-release fertiliser as a top-dressing, then simply prune back any long shoots on the oleander and cut down the pelargonium and sage by at least half. This may seem drastic but will allow the plants to regenerate good, healthy growth and maintain the pleasing balance of shape and size.

Without the help of a greenhouse there are still two options. One is to remove all the plants. Choisya and sage can be either potted and stood in a sheltered spot outside or planted in the garden. The two tender plants will have to be potted and brought indoors into a cool, bright position. The plants can be brought together again the following June or live their separate lives. Alternatively, remove only the tender plants and replace with small hardy evergreens, winter-flowering pansies and spring bulbs which will turn this versatile arrangement into a joy for the winter.

**PLANTS**

1 Three spider plants (*Chlorophytum comosum* 'Vittatum').
2 Two salmon-pink tuberous begonias.

**CONTAINER** Terracotta container from Knollys Nursery measuring 12 inches (30.5 cm) high and 12 inches (30.5 cm) diameter.

**POSITION** Will do well in both sun and shade.

**V**ery often the effect of using just two different types of plant rather than a great mixture can be striking. I find this combination particularly attractive for its contrasts. The begonias have a solid roundness to them which is admirably offset by the spiky foliage of the spider plant.

Plant the container up in spring. The most effective type of tuberous begonia to use is the 'Nonstop' which is free-flowering yet will not become tall and straggly. For those geared up to propagating their own plants from seed, they are available from most well-known seed companies and need an early December to February start under glass in the gentle heat of a propagating case. They are easily found for sale at garden centres along with all other kinds of bedding plant. Provide a good layer of drainage in the bottom of the container and plant into John Innes No. 2 compost with added peat and grit or a mixture of equal amounts of John Innes No. 2 and a peat-based compost. Do not risk standing outside until late May or early June as both spider plants and begonias are tender.

The success of this combination is not only aesthetic. I have seen both plant ingredients perform well in a shady, north-facing position although a sunny one is equally acceptable. Although the container should never be allowed to dry out, there is a certain amount of drought tolerance not shared by more fibrous-rooted plants. A weekly liquid feed will be of benefit and will ensure a good succession of flowers. Dead-head the begonias regularly.

Before the danger of autumnal frosts the arrangement will have to be taken apart for the winter. While most tuberous begonias will die down and can be dried off to be stored until spring, Nonstop is worth potting up to be brought indoors as a flowering houseplant. When they finally wear themselves out, throw them away and buy or grow new ones for next year. Spider plants, too, can be potted for house or greenhouse. Trim off dead leaves, stems and excess roots. These are fleshy and often run riot so that they need restricting before they will fit into a conventional pot. Either these mature plants or smaller ones grown on from plantlets can be used in the following year's container.

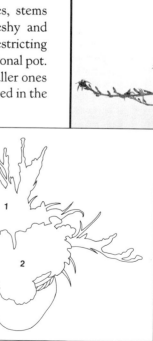

## PLANTS

1 One red-flowered Indian shot (*Canna indica* 'Purpurea').
2 Two hosta.
3 Three *Sedum spathulifolium* 'Purpureum'.

**CONTAINER** Swag and Acanthus Pot from Wichford Pottery measuring 15½ inches (39.5 cm) high and 22 inches (56 cm) diameter.

**POSITION** Preferably sunny or at least receiving sun for part of the day.

**C**anna are exotic tender plants which will lend a touch of flamboyance to the garden. There is a wide choice, the plant represented here having small flowers but attractive, shiny, bronze-red foliage. Other varieties have much showier flowers in shades of pink, red, orange and yellow (*see below for stockist*), and some even have variegated leaves. Choice of container is important, so that it is in scale with the height of the plant. This chunky, dark terracotta pot is heavily ornamented with swags and acanthus leaves which have decorated ornaments and buildings right back to Greek and Roman times. Cannas would look striking on their own, the surface topped off with large expanded clay pebbles to give a stylish finish. However, the greyish-blue, rounded leaves of hosta and purplish, succulent foliage of sedum are complementary and will not smother the decorated pot.

Plant in early spring, potting the fleshy rhizomes of the canna up and giving them a warm 60°F (15°C) to bring them into growth. Once established, they can be planted into the container with the other plants, using a compost of three parts John Innes No. 3 to one of moist peat and half of grit. Alternatively, mix equal amounts of John Innes No. 3 with a peat-based compost. Do not stand them outside until late May or early June. Keep well watered throughout the summer and liquid-feed fortnightly.

At summer's end, the container will have to be dismantled as the canna will need to over-winter in frost-free conditions. Pot the clump into a pot, reduce watering and allow the foliage to die down before cutting most of it away. Keep plants very much on the dry side, giving the occasional watering just to prevent them drying out completely. The following spring, water the dormant rhizomes, move them into a warmer place and watch for new growth. This is the best time to divide the rhizomes into smaller sections to be potted individually. As well as being used in containers, spare plants will grow and flower in open borders but will need lifting again for winter.

Suppliers of cannas often stock other interesting fleshy-rooted or bulbous plants. Alternatives might include agapanthus, with tall heads of blue, white or purple flowers, the South African pineapple bulb, *Eucomis bicolor*, with speckled stems of long-lasting, maroon-tinged, cream-coloured flowers crowned by a tuft of leaves, lilies (for summer), and *Nerine bowdenii* (for autumn).

### Stockist

Canna from Jacques Amand Ltd, The Nurseries, 145 Clamp Hill, Stanmore, Middx HA7 3JS.

**PLANTS**

1 One lemon balm (*Melissa officinalis*).
2 Two purple sage (*Salvia officinalis* 'Purpurascens').
3 Two sweet marjoram (*Origanum majoranum*).
4 One golden thyme (*Thymus* × *citriodorus* 'Aureus').
5 One rosemary (*Rosmarinus officinalis*).
6 One French tarragon (*Artemisia dracunculus*).

**CONTAINER** Round terracotta bowl from Secret Garden measuring 8½ inches (20 cm) deep by 20 inches (51 cm) diameter.

**POSITION** Plenty of sun.

A selection of herbs makes a pleasantly aromatic and useful container. I like to plant mostly the culinary types. Not only does this keep me well supplied but the continual robbing of shoot tips keeps growth rounded and compact.

Plant the container in spring, using your favourites but giving some thought to the shape and structure of one herb against the other. There are coloured-leaved and variegated types which bring relief from plain green. A John Innes No. 2 with added peat and grit or a mixture of equal amounts of John Innes No. 2 and a peat-based compost would be ideal. Once established, keep well watered and liquid-feed every week if you are cutting a lot from the plants.

Lemon balm releases a wonderful perfume when its stems and leaves are crushed. Look out for the golden-leaved form. Sage is useful for scattering over sausages about to be grilled, adding to stuffings and to pasta dishes containing bacon. Apart from the purple-leaved form there is *S.o.* 'Icterina' which is variegated and *S.o.* 'Tricolor' with grey-green, white and pink leaves. Marjoram is a useful addition to many recipes, as is thyme. There are plain, silver- and golden-leaved forms as well as many species and named varieties.

Rosemary can grow into a large shrub and must have shoots continuously removed to keep it within bounds. I use masses to flavour any kind of lamb dish, especially to sprinkle on chops for grilling. If you run out of ideas, simply throw stems on to the barbecue for their delicious scent. Tarragon looks fragile and certainly can be temperamental to grow. It must have a warm, sunny position and needs watching so that other herbs do not smother it.

As the shrubby herbs have a tendency to become woody with time, they may not look as good for a second year. Cuttings can be taken of sage, tarragon, rosemary and marjoram during spring or summer. Lemon balm can be split up in spring or autumn to make smaller clumps. Most of the herbs should overwinter to be trimmed back in spring if kept in a sheltered spot where the compost will not be frozen for too long a time.

**PLANTS**

1 Five black-eyed Susan (*Thunbergia alata*).

2 Three blue petunias.

**CONTAINER** Large pot with white glaze from Secret Garden measuring 10½ inches (27 cm) high and 15½ inches (39 cm) diameter.

**POSITION** Full sun.

A lot of fun can be had by planting containers of climbing plants and training them up wigwams of canes. The most suitable are annual climbers raised from seed. In reality, some of the best choices are not annuals at all but tender perennial climbers grown as annuals which, at the end of the season, usually succumb to the first hard frost. It is to this category that *Thunbergia alata* belongs. A native of tropical Africa, it is popular for the cheerful orange, yellow or white flowers with black centres. Most seed is sold as 'Susie Mixed' and if you want as many orange flowers as possible, it pays to grow quite a few, wait until they begin flowering, then choose the strongest colours to plant up. Although thunbergia would be effective on its own, a few blue petunias have been added for contrast. Lobelia or felicia might also be pleasant alternatives.

The container is best planted at the end of May using well-grown plants sown in February or March, or plants bought from a garden centre. John Innes No. 2 compost with added peat and grit or a mixture of equal amounts of John Innes No. 2 and a peat-based compost will be ideal. Having planted, push four approximately 5-foot canes around the edge of the pot, then tie the tops in together. Wait for the plants to establish (about three weeks) before beginning weekly liquid feeds with a well-balanced fertiliser to encourage plenty of flowers. They have a natural tendency to climb and will not need much encouragement. When watering, squirt up under the leaves to deter red spider mite to which they might be prone in a hot, dry summer. However, avoid wetting the foliage in full sun as this can cause scorching.

Alternative plants include *Eccremocarpus scaber*, the Chilean glory vine, with bright, orange-red tubular flowers. Mixtures like 'Mardi Gras Mixed' or 'Anglia Hybrids' extend the colour range to red, pink, yellow and bicolours. *Cobaea scandens*, the cup and saucer plant, is easy to grow from seed and amazingly rampant. However, you will have to wait until September or October for its curious purplish-blue flowers to appear. *Cardiospermum halicacabum* may not have showy flowers but is worth growing for its inflated seed pods, giving it the common name of love-in-a-puff. Smaller climbers include the Chilean bell vine (*Rhodochiton atrosanguineum*). *Asarina scandens* and *A.* 'Ruby' (new from Thompson and Morgan) may not be too rampant but the gorgeous pink trumpet-flowered *A. barcalaiana* can be quite vigorous.

*Impomoea* 'Heavenly Blue' is a true annual with flowers like a giant blue bellbind. Climbing nasturtium, canary creeper (*Tropaeolum peregrinum*) and even sweet peas can be sown straight into the container in which they will flower.

**PLANTS**

1 One *Artemisia* 'Powis Castle'.
2 Two white zonal pelargonium.
3 Two white tuberous begonias.
4 Two white trailing Verbena (*Verbena tenuisecta* 'Alba').

**CONTAINER** White stone pot from Knollys Nursery measuring 17 inches (43 cm) high and 15 inches (38 cm) diameter.

**POSITION** Full sun or with sun for most of the day.

Some containers are effective because they are brimming with colour, while others, like this quiet combination of silver and white, are equally successful on account of their subtlety. The most effective position for this container is the sunniest place in the garden, where the colours will create an illusion of coolness.

Planting time is spring. If you have a frost-free greenhouse, take advantage of the early appearance of bedding plants in the garden centres, to plant early. Stand the container outside in late May or early June when the danger of a late frost has passed. Alternatively, plant up at this time; the plants will quickly grow and knit together. Place a layer of expanded clay pebbles in the base of the pot and use a John Innes No. 2 compost with added peat and grit or a mixture of equal amounts of John Innes No. 2 and a peat-based compost. Remember to leave a good inch (2 to 3 cm) gap at the top to allow for watering. Once the plants have become established and begin growing strongly (about one month), liquid-feed fortnightly until the end of summer.

Height and foliage interest is provided by artemisia. There are several of these shrubby perennials which can be used to similar effect. *Artemisia arborescens* has aromatic, silvery foliage but is not frost hardy unless you choose the variety 'Faith Raven'. *A. absinthium* 'Lambrook Silver' is very similar and hardy as is *A.* 'Powis Castle'. All will produce yellow flower heads during summer, which can be removed if you feel they spoil the colour harmony of the display. The middle ground is occupied by white zonal pelargoniums. You can buy them or raise your own plants from seed, choosing an all-white F1 variety like 'Ringo White' from Dobies.

The more sumptuous white flowers of the tuberous begonias supplement those of the pelargoniums. The 'Nonstop' varieties are ideal. Finally, a trailing plant of some description is a must. *Verbena tenuisecta* 'Alba' is a particularly attractive and delicate verbena. If it proves difficult to find, look for *V.* 'White Knight' or supplement with white trailing lobelia. Sow some at home in case only the mixed or blue varieties are on offer. *Lobelia* 'White Fountains' is a good white trailer obtainable from Suttons and Mr Fothergill's.

Instead of throwing the plants on to the compost heap at the end of the season, all but lobelia can be kept for the following year. Cuttings of artemisia, verbena and pelargonium rooted towards the end of summer and the old plants potted and cut back, can be over-wintered in a frost-free greenhouse. Tuberous begonias can be dried off and stored frost-free to be started off again the following February or March. The main plant of artemisia, if a hardy types, could even be planted in a sunny position in well-drained soil outside.

### PLANTS

**1** Three pale salmon pink zonal geranium (*Pelargonium* 'Century Light Salmon').

**2** Three pink ivy-leaved geranium (*Pelargonium* 'Roi des Balcons Rose').

**CONTAINER** Basket Flowerpot from Wichford Pottery measuring 6½ inches (16.5 cm) high and 14 inches (35.5 cm) diameter.

**POSITION** Full sun, or at least receiving sun for part of the day.

Most gardeners refer to these plants as 'geraniums' but botanically they should be called pelargoniums. The most popular for summer containers are zonal pelargoniums and pretty, trailing ivy-leaved or balcony pelargoniums. This terracotta tub is a pleasant mixture of both, which, stood on the edge of a patio or set to trail over the edge of some steps, should provide a generous display.

Plant up in spring when all danger of frost is past, crocking the bottom of the container and using a John Innes No. 2 compost with added peat and grit or a mixture of equal parts of John Innes No. 2 and a peat-based compost. After about one month, when the plants seem to be growing strongly, give fortnightly liquid feeds. Remove faded flowers and dead leaves from the plants to encourage more flowers and prevent rotting of foliage in damp summers.

While our container shows the type of pelargoniums you can easily buy from any garden centre, you can also seek out the more unusual species and varieties by finding a pelargonium specialist and sending off for their catalogue (*see below for stockists*). They will send you rooted cuttings through the post in the spring. Choose at least five plants which you think will make a good combination. P. 'Lady Ilchester' with double flowers of soft pink or P. 'Mabel Grey' with strongly lemon-scented leaves will make tall plants. For contrast, choose a yellow-leaved variety like the compact P. 'Elsie Portas' or P. *fragrans* with delicate, pine-scented, sage-green foliage and tiny white flowers. Or choose a coloured-leaved type like P. 'Mrs Pollock', a golden tricolour with vermilion flowers.

I like to increase my stock in the summer by taking cuttings which will happily overwinter in a frost-free greenhouse. Before autumn frosts, lift and pot the old plants, cutting them back by a good half. Given a thorough prune-back in spring, they can be used again.

### Stockists

Fibrex Nurseries Ltd (Pelargonium Catalogue), Honeybourne Road, Pebworth, Nr Stratford-on-Avon, CV37 8XT.

The Vernon Geranium Nursery, Cuddington Way, Cheam, Sutton, Surrey SM2 7JB (mail order only).

## PLANTS

1 One New Zealand flax (*Phormium tenax* 'Purpureum').
2 Five red petunias.
3 Five white petunias.

**CONTAINER** Small Versailles Vase from Haddonstone measuring 27 inches (68.5 cm) high and 21 inches (53.5 cm) diameter.

**POSITION** Bright, sunny and sheltered. The phormium, particularly, needs a bright, sheltered spot during winter.

This elegant composition of phormium and petunia reminds me of the formal bedding-out areas and stone planters displayed on the terraces of large country houses around the latter part of the nineteenth century. Heckfield Place in Hampshire, for instance, still boasts beautiful, if rather dilapidated, stone planters and beds set into a lawn. In its heyday, when head gardener William Wildsmith was in charge, imaginative plants like hardy ferns, ornamental cabbage, fatsia, abutilon, agave and indeed phormium would have been used. This is not too grand for today's smaller garden. Most of us have, or would like, a patio area close to the house or where the sun shines most. This usually becomes the formal part of the garden and can be decorated with suitably exotic, flamboyant containers. Alternatively, an elegant pedestal planting can also be used to draw the eye down a path or vista.

Planting time would be late May or early June for the benefit of the petunias which would not tolerate late frosts. Place a good layer of crocks or expanded clay pebbles at the base of the container and pot the phormium into a mixture of John Innes No. 2 with added peat and grit or a mixture of equal parts of John Innes No. 2 and a peat-based compost. The petunias can be added afterwards around the top.

*Phormium tenax* is a reasonably hardy plant with dark green, sword-shaped leaves, creating a subtropical effect. I like the combination of the purple-leaved form with the bold red and white of the petunias. Sometimes, during summer, a thick flower stalk will be produced bearing reddish flowers. If you are feeling reckless you could choose one of the less hardy colour variations like 'Aurora' which has leaves striped with red, pink, bronze and yellow, 'Dazzler', with bright pink and dark bronze leaves, or 'Veitchii' with leaves striped with creamy white. As the species, in particular, will come safely through most winters, it could be left in the container indefinitely, preferably in a sheltered spot. Eventually the clump will become too large and will need to be lifted and divided.

Keep the container well watered and give fortnightly liquid feeds during summer. Dead-head the petunias regularly, removing them when autumn frosts have taken their toll. Top up with fresh compost and spruce up with winter- or spring-flowering pansies, winter-flowering heathers or foliage plants like large ivies combined, perhaps, with a single colour of hybrid crocus. In spring, when the plants of winter interest are cleared away, repeat this top-dressing with the addition of some slow-release fertiliser.

## PLANTS

1 One *Artemisia* 'Powis Castle'.
2 Three light-blue petunia.
3 Two yellow marguerites
   (*Argyranthemum* 'Jenny').
4 Three Swan River daisies (*Brachycome* 'Tinkerbell').
5 One variegated ground ivy (*Glechoma hederacea* 'Variegata').
6 One *Potentilla fruticosa*.

**CONTAINER** Haddonstone Warwick Castle Urn measuring 20 inches (51 cm) high, 16 inches (41 cm) diameter at the top and 22 inches (56 cm) diameter at the widest.

**POSITION** Sun for at least part of the day.

This beautifully planted pedestal urn would look wonderful at the end of a vista, leading the eye down to the bottom of a path or the end of a lawn. Containers can be used to play tricks in a garden. A path leading to a compost heap could look as if it were structured entirely for the purpose of inspecting this urn, with the heap tucked well round the corner. Blue and yellow is a happy combination of colours for plants, especially with the complement of silver and variegated foliage. Note how the plants are chosen to grow into a pyramid shape in scale with the proportions of the urn. A small plinth would be needed to raise the trailing plants off the ground.

Plant in spring, placing outside in late May/early June. A John Innes No. 2 with added peat and grit or a mixture of equal amounts of John Innes No. 2 and a peat-based compost would be ideal. Keep well watered during summer and liquid-feed every fortnight from the end of June. Dead-head the marguerites, petunias and brachycome assiduously to ensure a good succession of colour.

*Artemisia* 'Powis Castle' is an invaluable foliage plant to add height and colour contrast to containers. In the autumn, when the rest of the plants have been moved on, it could be planted into the garden or left in place to be dressed up with foliage, colour and bulbs for winter and spring interest. Lilac or blue petunias are available from garden centres in single pots or mixed boxes. Alternatively, they are easy to raise from seed. Choose a variety like 'Daddy Blue' from Mr Fothergill's or 'Resisto Blue' from Unwins.

*Argyranthemum* have become very popular in recent years so that most garden centres have a good selection including 'Jenny'. Cuttings can be taken during summer to be kept in a frost-free greenhouse for the following year. Variegated glechoma is such a good trailing plant for urns and baskets as it takes up very little prime space in the top. It is incredible how much growth one plant will make in a season and cuttings are easy to root. The plants usually need winter frost protection to survive for another year. Brachyscome is another plant enjoying recent popularity. Pots of plants are readily available and it can be raised from seed. *Brachyscome* 'Purple Splendour' from Mr Fothergill's or *Iberidifolia* 'Mixed' from Unwins would be good choices. The potentilla, added to give height and bulk as well as a succession of yellow flowers, is hardy and could be planted in the garden in the autumn.

## PLANTS

1 One standard bay tree (*Laurus nobilis*).
2 Two white zonal pelargoniums.
3 Two purple heliotropes (*Heliotropium* 'Princess Marina').
4 Eight white impatiens.
5 One pick-a-back plant (*Tolmiea menziesii* 'Taff's Gold').
6 One variegated hosta (*Hosta montana* 'Aureomarginata').

**CONTAINER** Large wooden barrel measuring 13½ inches (34 cm) high and 25 inches (63.5 cm) diameter. Make sure there are good drainage holes drilled in the base. Should you need to move the barrel around, fix castors on the bottom before planting.

**POSITION** Sun or semi-shade.

This container would make a grand focal point in any garden, with its stately standard bay tree and underplanting of white, purple and green.

Plant the container in spring, but, as most of the plants are tender, it should not be stood outside until late May or early June. Place some expanded clay pebbles in the base, then use a compost of John Innes No. 3 mixed with extra peat and grit, or a mixture of equal amounts of John Innes No. 3 and a peat-based compost. As this is a large container to fill, you could add the remains of an old grow bag, or good garden soil, to help bulk it up. Position the bay tree carefully in the centre so that when compost is firmed down around it, the top of the root ball will be at exactly the correct height to allow for watering. Then arrange the other plants around it. Keep well watered during summer and give fortnightly liquid feeds once established.

A standard bay is not cheap to buy but should last for many years if kept sheltered during winter in a protected part of the garden, or under glass. Keep the head of the bay in shape by trimming wayward shoots back and remove any suckers from the long stem. Watch out for scale-insect attack to which it is prone. It is possible to grow a standard from a good, straight cutting. The process is similar to that used for forming a standard fuchsia. Tie the main stem to a cane, taking off any side shoots that form along it. Once the stem has reached the desired height, allow it to grow another 6 inches (15 cm) before stopping it (pinching out the tip). The side shoots that form at the top should be stopped repeatedly at four leaves until the head has formed.

The plants beneath should be easy to find or grow. White impatiens can be grown from seed, for example 'Accent White' from Dobies or 'Tempo White' from Thompson and Morgan. Similarly with the pelargonium, often listed under geranium, for example 'Gala White' from Unwins. Heliotrope can be raised from seed but often takes a long while to begin flowering. Once you have the plants, summer cuttings can be taken and the new plants overwintered in a frost-free greenhouse. Older plants can be pruned in spring to keep them compact. Hostas are usually abundant in garden centres or a small clump can be lifted from plants in the garden. Tolmiea is sometimes found in the houseplant section of the garden centre. At the end of summer, it can be potted and brought indoors. Plantlets form on mature leaves and can be grown for new plants.

# HANGING BASKETS

Hanging baskets and wall planters can transform the plainest of buildings. Unfortunately they are vulnerable to drying out, sometimes requiring water twice a day during a hot spell in summer. Well cared for, watered and fed, a summer hanging basket should look good right through to the first frosts of autumn.

There is no need to go without colour in winter. Plant up another set of baskets for winter and spring interest. A mixture of evergreen foliage, winter and spring flowerers and spring bulbs will cheer up the dullest days. At every stage of planning a hanging basket, thought should be given to moisture retention. Solid plastic baskets probably hold more moisture but are less attractive and plants cannot be poked through the sides. For our photographs we have used wire baskets with a lining of sphagnum moss. Fitted liners of pressed peat can be used but they look ugly at first and prevent plants being tucked in the sides unless holes are cut. Special fitted liners of spongy material are easy to use and plants can be fitted in the sides. A very thin cosmetic layer of moss between the basket and liner will mask its rather unreal colours. Similar, but more aesthetically pleasing, are liners of coconut fibre.

Before adding compost, a saucer or extra liner of polythene placed in the base will help retain moisture. Build up compost gradually, poking trailing plants through the sides and sitting the roots on the compost, firming more around. Finish off with the plants to go in the top but remember to leave a gap for watering.

Special hanging basket composts usually contain moisture-retaining agents. However, one can buy these agents separately from garden centres or by mail order. Peat-based compost is usually the favourite. For those wanting to cut down on the use of peat, try one of the peat alternatives, add extra peat and sharp sand to a John Innes No. 2 or mix equal amounts of John Innes No. 2 with a peat-based compost.

The best way to ensure that summer baskets are well watered is to make this as easy as possible. There are various hand pumps and bottles with long tubes attached, most of which are rather laborious to use. One of the best ideas is to have the basket on a lowering device so that it can be pulled down for watering. Hosepipe lances will give extra reach. Some can be fitted with cartridges of fertiliser to make liquid feeding easier.

Apart from the combinations of plants shown, single-subject baskets can be most effective. Try planting a basket full of pale pink impatiens for summer or a mass of blue pansies for winter/spring.

**PLANTS**

1 Five bulbs of *Narcissus* 'Tête-à-Tête'.
2 One pink winter-flowering heather (*Erica carnea* 'Springwood Pink').
3 One variegated lesser periwinkle (*Vinca minor* 'Aureovariegata').
4 Two *Ophiopogon planiscapus nigrescens.*
5 Three golden-yellow winter/spring-flowering pansies.
6 One partridge berry or checkerberry (*Gaultheria procumbens*).
7 One *Hedera helix* 'Glacier'.
8 Five bulbs of *Crocus* 'Remembrance'.

**CONTAINER** Hanging basket 15 inches (38 cm) in diameter.

**POSITION** Sun or semi-shade. A north-facing position would be acceptable.

This combination is a great favourite of mine as it contains all that one could want from a basket planted for winter and spring interest – evergreen and variegated foliage, berries and flowers all packed in together. Even in summer the arrangement is interesting enough to retain in full view. I have found that the plants look better after establishing themselves for two or more seasons.

Plant up in autumn, lining the basket with moss and using a compost for acid-loving plants which will suit the gaultheria and not bother the rest. Although planting in the sides of a basket is a good idea for summer, I find that the drying effect of cold winter winds is usually too much for small plants trying to establish themselves. Keep all the planting in the top, poking the crocus and narcissus bulbs in around the other plants before finally filling in and firming. Remember to leave a margin at the top for watering. Liquid-feed monthly between May and October with a well-balanced fertiliser. After the bulbs have finished flowering, living with their foliage for at least the following six weeks will ensure flowers for next spring. Remove the pansies for the summer as they will straggle over the other plants, and in autumn give the ivy and vinca a trim if necessary. Carefully dig into the surface, pushing roots and bulbs to either side, to accommodate three new pansies.

Gaultheria is an attractive little evergreen from north-east America, which bears small, pinkish-white, bell-shaped flowers in July and August followed by red winter berries. Given the right compost and watered regularly during summer, preferably with soft water, one plant should spread into a clump during the life of the basket. The ophiopogon, too, will send up new plants. Ivies and vincas are good trailing plants for a winter basket. Choice of narcissus, crocus and pansies can be a personal one as long as the narcissus are short growers.

**PLANTS**

1 One variegated ivy (*Hedera helix* 'Glacier').
2 One plain green ivy (*Hedera helix* 'Pittsburgh').
3 One variegated ivy (*Hedera helix* 'Goldchild').
4 Five Universal pansies.
5 Three winter-flowering heathers (*Erica* × *darleyensis* 'Silberschmelze').
6 Fifteen bulbs or three pots of grape hyacinths (*Muscari armeniacum*).
7 Three pots or 15 bulbs of small daffodils (*Narcissus* 'Topolino).

**CONTAINER** Hanging basket measuring 16 inches (40.5 cm) in diameter.

**POSITION** Sun or semi-shade. A north-facing position would be suitable.

The same hanging baskets which burgeoned with summer-flowering petunias, begonias and lobelias could be used again to brighten up the house in winter but so often are not. This basket should be attractive from autumn to spring with evergreen foliage, winter flower colour and spring bulbs.

The ideal planting time is autumn, and it is perfectly feasible to use the basket and old liner from a summer planting. I would avoid planting in the sides where plants can dry out and die off in winter. The ivies will adequately mask the sides, tumbling over the rim of the basket. Before finally filling and firming in, nestle the bulbs down into the compost around the other plants. Narcissus should be covered so that their tips or 'noses' are just under the surface, the grape hyacinths planted 2 inches (5 cm) deep. Water in and remember to check regularly, as even in winter baskets can dry out. Should there be a prolonged spell of freezing conditions with cold winds, take the basket down and stand it on a pot somewhere sheltered. Although the plants are hardy, their roots are more exposed to cold, drying winds than if they were in the ground.

Should you run out of steam in the autumn but be looking for something creative to do in the garden in January, this container could be planted then. Garden centres should begin to sell pots of bulbs around this time, and although you will have to use what is available, the results should be as good. If it proves impossible to fit whole pots of bulbs between the other plants, carefully divide them up, trying to disturb the roots as little as possible.

There is some mileage to be had by not disturbing this arrangement once planted. By the end of May when flowers have finished and you are anxious to put up a basket for summer, consider saving this one intact for the following autumn. I have kept a basket going for three years now, sitting it on top of an urn for the summer where the foliage of ivies and heather provides some interest. I usually pull up the pansies, replacing them with fresh ones in the autumn, while the bulbs should continue to come up every spring. The foliage could even be used to cover an old tree stump, propping the basket on the top and letting the ivies take over. Water and liquid-feed well during summer, then trim the plants back in autumn to smarten them up for their turn in the limelight.

**PLANTS**

1 Six *Mimulus longiflorus*.
2 Five red impatiens.
3 Three golden creeping Jenny
   (*Lysimachia nummularia* 'Aurea').

**CONTAINER** Hanging basket measuring 16 inches (40.5 cm) in diameter.

**POSITION** Will tolerate shade. Suitable for a north-facing aspect.

**M**ost bedding plants which do well in hanging baskets prefer bright sun to reach their full potential. However, there are some bright and lovely flowering and foliage plants which will tolerate or even enjoy a shadier place. The gloomier north-facing aspect of a building is the one that really needs cheering up with some pretty hanging baskets and this is just one example of what can be achieved.

Plant the basket in spring for a summer display. As most of the plants are tender it must not be hung in position until late May or early June. Using a special hanging basket compost, plant up in layers from the base so that the creeping Jenny and some of the impatiens can be planted through the bottom and sides of the basket. More impatiens and the mimulus can be planted in the top. Once the plants have established themselves give weekly liquid feeds of a well-balanced fertiliser. One advantage of a hanging basket in shade is that it will not need so much water as its sun-loving counterparts but, nevertheless, check it regularly.

All mimulus can tolerate shade. Most straightforward to find are those that have been bred as bedding plants known as monkey musk or monkey flowers which can easily be raised from seed. However, there are some species worth tracking down as plants, which are unusual and often softer in colour. *M. aurantiacus* (*M. glutinosa*) is one of these with pale orange flowers, making a shrubby plant which should tolerate a mild winter outside. In the basket is *M. longiflorus* with long, tubular flowers of a deeper orange colour. This, too, should be hardy if left outside in a sheltered place. The other advantage these have over their seed-raised cousins is added height which makes a nice pinnacle to the basket arrangement. Having acquired stock, I would propagate by summer cuttings which can be over-wintered, perhaps in a cold frame, for next year's display.

Impatiens are easy enough to buy or grow. All are tolerant of shade and will perform better if not scorched to death against a south-facing wall. A basket planted just with impatiens, even of a single colour, can be most effective.

I love trailing plants cascading from the bottom of a basket. As many of the choices need light to grow well, especially variegated and silver-leaved kinds, then choose creeping Jenny for its shade tolerance. More often grown as a shade-loving, creeping groundcover plant which spreads long stems of rounded leaves across the ground, it smothers weeds and produces small, bright yellow flowers. As its stems usually root naturally as they grow, cuttings of this hardy plant are easy to root. I would take summer cuttings to be grown on in pots outside for baskets the following year.

### PLANTS

1 One *Senecio bicolor cineraria* (formerly *Cineraria maritima* 'Silver Dust').
2 Three pink tuberous begonias.
3 Five pale pink impatiens.
4 Five *Helichrysum petiolare*.
5 Three *Glechoma hederacea* 'Variegata' syn. *Nepeta glechoma* 'Variegata'.

**CONTAINER** Hanging basket measuring 16 inches (40.5 cm) in diameter.

**POSITION** Sun or semi-shade. Would tolerate a north-facing position.

This basket makes me think of Cheltenham, where excellent examples of trailing hanging baskets are to be seen every summer. Of course, there are many plants that could be used in such an arrangement but it is the balance and shape which are so appealing here. The top of the basket reaches a peak with the silver-leaved cineraria. A round, balanced middle section is pleasantly achieved with the silver of the helichrysum, enhanced by the pale pink flowers of impatiens and the other shades of pink of the tuberous begonias. Finally, festoons of foliage are provided by the glechoma.

Plant the basket in spring, not hanging it up outside until late May or early June. Use a special hanging basket compost which should have greater moisture-retaining properties. Build layers up slowly from the base, planting first the glechoma, then impatiens and helichrysum in the sides, finishing with the begonias and senecio in the top. Remember to leave a gap in the top for watering, creating a sturdy rim with the moss. Once the plants are established in the compost and have obviously started to grow, give a couple of high-nitrogen liquid feeds to boost growth, before moving on to twice-weekly feeds of high-potash fertiliser to keep the begonias and impatiens flowering well. Deadhead the begonias regularly to keep plenty of flowers coming.

For those who prefer to grow their own bedding and container plants, senecio and impatiens can be grown from seed. Single colours should be easy to find like 'Accent Pink' from Dobies or 'Super Elfin Salmon Blush' from Mr Fothergill's. 'Nonstop' tuberous begonias can be raised from seed but this is very small and therefore only for the experienced or adventurous. It may be difficult to find seed of single colours, so select the colours you want from potted plants in the garden centre.

During summer, cuttings can be taken from helichrysum and glechoma to be overwintered frost-free and used the following year. However, this can often be more trouble than it is worth as plants are readily available at garden centres every spring. Helichrysum cuttings root better if they are not covered with a plastic or polythene lid as their felty leaves can easily rot.

Tuberous begonias can be taken out of the basket in autumn, tucked up in boxes of compost until they have died down, then shaken dry and stored frost-free for the winter. In March, rub off their old roots and start into growth, planting shallow side upwards in some peat or compost in a warm place. The basket, having been completely dismantled in autumn, can be planted up straightaway with plants for winter and spring interest.

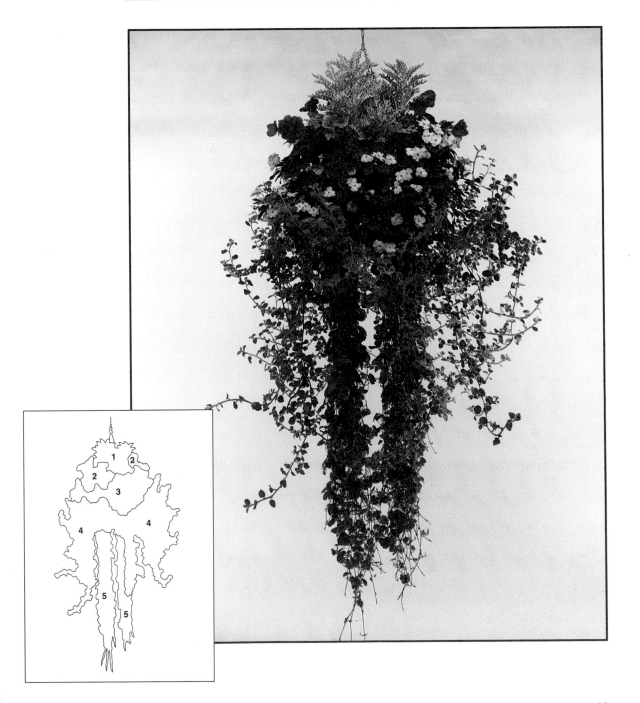

## PLANTS

1  One *Senecio bicolor cineraria* (formerly *Cineraria maritima* 'Silver Dust').
2  Three variegated blue marguerites (*Felicia amelloides* in variegated form, sometimes called *F. capensis* 'Variegata').
3  Ten blue trailing lobelia.

**CONTAINER** Hanging basket measuring 16 inches (40.5 cm) in diameter.

**POSITION** Full sun.

At first glance, this basket might be considered to be overly subtle. However, within the context of a colourful, flowery garden, its cool silvers and blues will make a welcome rest for the eye.

Plant the basket in spring but don't hang the container outside until all danger of frost is past. When planting, build up layers from the bottom so that lots of lobelia plants can be accommodated around the sides. Senecio and felicia can easily be planted in the top, remembering to leave a gap for watering. Use a special hanging basket compost which should have greater moisture-retaining properties. When plants are established, liquid-feed weekly with a high-nitrogen liquid feed. However, by mid-June this should be changed to a high-potash fertiliser to encourage flowering.

*Senecio bicolor cineraria* is a large plant which will fill the top of the basket with its silvery leaves. Should your plant appear spindly, nip out the tips to encourage branching. Those keen to grow their own plants can do so from seed sown in February or March. Felicia is a South African plant which has become more readily available in recent years. A tender perennial with lax, bushy habit, it can be propagated by summer cuttings which then need to be over-wintered frost-free. In our basket the stems radiate outwards, the blue daisy-like flowers flung out on long stalks.

Other plants offering this sort of colour combination include *Helichrysum petiolare*, a robust and spreading silver-leaved trailing plant, *Brachycome* 'Purple Splendour', one of the Swan River daisies which will create splashes of blue around the sides. *Nolana* 'Bluebird' and 'Shooting Stars' can be raised from seed. Originating from desert regions of Chile, nolana should be more drought-tolerant than lobelia. Round blue flowers with white and yellow centres are most attractive. Trailing *Convolvulus sabatius* has silvery leaves and blue flowers. A good idea would be to plant one or two *Ipomoea* 'Heavenly Blue' plants (easily raised from seed) in the top. These will climb up the chains and hook, providing late summer colour with their blue saucer-shaped flowers.

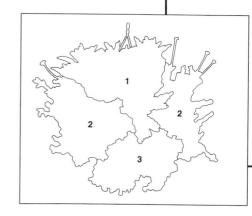

**PLANTS**

1 Five *Pelargonium* 'Silipen'.
2 Five blue trailing lobelia.
3 Three double red-flowered nasturtium (*Tropaeolum* 'Hermine Grashof').
4 Four black-eyed Susan (*Thunbergia alata*).

**CONTAINER** Basket measuring 16 inches (40.5 cm) in diameter.

**POSITION** Full sun or sun for most of the day.

This basket does not pretend to be subtle, its predominant colours being red and blue. Thunbergia adds a more gentle shade of orange but could come in paler orange, white or yellow. Ideally, these climbers should be more predominant, not only trailing down but climbing up the chains.

Plant up in spring but do not hang the basket outside until late May or early June. A moisture-retaining potting compost specially formulated for hanging baskets would be ideal. Build up from the bottom, planting lobelia and double nasturtiums into the base and sides. At least two plants of thunbergia should be placed near the bottom so that they will trail down. Plant the pelargoniums in the top along with some of the nasturtiums and lobelia, then position one or two thunbergia so that they will quickly begin to climb up the chains. Drying out must be avoided at all times. Feed the basket at first with high-nitrogen fertiliser to boost growth, changing to a high-potash fertiliser which will encourage flowering. During midsummer two feeds a week would not be too much. Should the plants begin to look jaded, a couple of nitrogen feeds during August will work wonders, encouraging new shoots bearing fresh flower buds.

The nasturtium used here is a double-flowered variety which has to be propagated by cuttings. Once plants have been acquired, a cool greenhouse can be used to overwinter stock plants or cuttings which root easily and can be taken in late summer. Once rooted, they will remain alive but grow very little during winter at about 40°F (5°C), bursting into fresh growth in spring. Virtually any compact, red-flowering geraniums could be used, including those grown from seed. Named varieties are worth propagating in late summer. If you have a greenhouse, lobelia and black-eyed Susan are easily grown from spring-sown seed. Strains like *Thunbergia alata* 'Susie' (Dobies) contain orange, white and yellow flowers with or without the black eye. Plants left over can be used as climbers in the garden or greenhouse.

Quite often, baskets which started off well at the beginning of the season will begin to look tatty, especially if watering has been neglected and clumps of lobelia have died off. This is where seed-sown nasturtiums come into their own. All you have to do is decide to be more thorough with the basket care, make sure the basket is well moistened once more, then push seeds into the compost. These will germinate and grow quickly, giving a beautiful late display and lengthening the life of the arrangement. You could choose brightly coloured 'Gleam Hybrids' (Dobies) or more subtle shades like 'Peach Melba' (Mr Fothergill's) or 'Strawberries and Cream' (Thompson and Morgan).

## PLANTS

1 Three yellow marguerites
  (*Argyranthemum* 'Jenny').
2 Seven white petunias.
3 Three slipper flowers (*Calceolaria* 'Sunshine').
4 Five *Bidens ferulifolia*.

**CONTAINER** Hanging basket measuring 16 inches (40.5 cm) in diameter.

**POSITION** Full sun or sun for most of the day.

A sunny combination of white and yellow flowers makes an interesting summer basketful. The effect here is certainly not compact or bold but looks rather as if the flowers have been individually arranged. Perhaps not a basket for the tidy-minded but nevertheless very attractive.

Plant up in spring for summer interest. The plants are not hardy, so do not risk hanging outside until all danger of frost is past at the end of May or beginning of June. Use a special hanging basket compost and build up layers from the bottom so that the bidens and some of the petunias can be planted into the sides. Fill up gradually around the young plants, positioning the rest into the top. Remember to leave a gap to allow for watering so that should the compost become dry, water will soak in rather than run off. Once the plants are established (about three weeks), liquid-feed every week with a well-balanced fertiliser.

'Jenny' is a particularly lovely marguerite with large, bright yellow, daisy-like flowers on a fairly tall plant. Having acquired stock, summer cuttings which will have to be over-wintered frost-free, will ensure plants for the following season. If only a few plants of the calceolaria are needed, this, too, can be propagated by summer cuttings. However, it can also be raised from seed (Suttons). Unlike the better-known large-flowered kinds of slipper flower, more commonly grown as pot plants, this is dainty, bearing clusters of jewel-like, bright golden-yellow flowers all summer. White petunias should be easy to come by and can easily be raised from seed. 'Resisto Pure White' (Dobies) is a multiflora variety as is 'Brass Band' (Dobies) which has a clear primrose-yellow centre, fading to white at the edges. This reflects the colours of the basket and might be an even better choice.

*Bidens ferulifolia* is a recently popular plant which adds to the collection of trailing plants available for baskets. Native to Mexico, it is a straggly perennial grown as a half-hardy annual represented in cultivation by the variety 'Golden Goddess' (seed from Thompson and Morgan or Chilterns). *Ferulifolia* means with fennel-like leaves and it is for these and its dainty yellow flowers that it has become popular for baskets. An easy plant to grow, it is a reliable performer, flowering all summer with some tolerance of shade and resistance to wet.

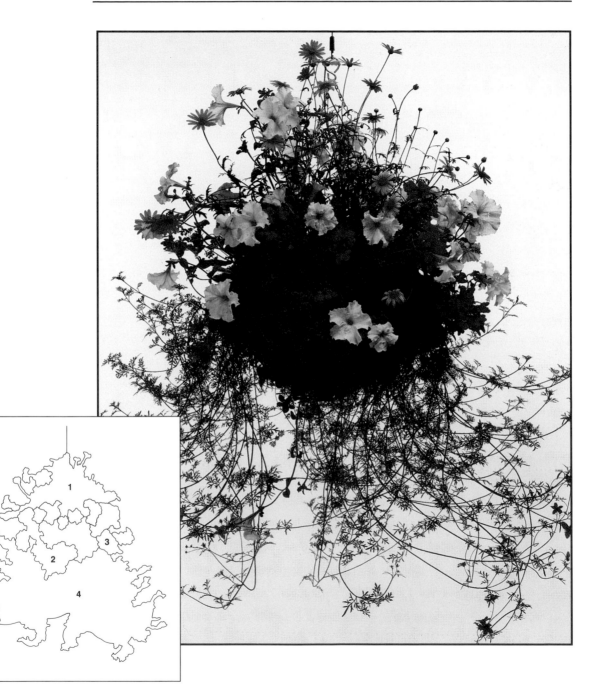

# WINDOW BOXES AND TROUGHS

Like, and often in conjunction with, hanging baskets, a well-chosen combination of the right container and plants will brighten up and enhance a building. Unfortunately not all houses, including my own, have a wide enough window ledge to accommodate even the slimmest of boxes. However, brackets can be fixed under the window, or on any part of the wall, onto which the box can sit. This has other advantages, in that taller plants can be used which would otherwise have obscured the window.

Before rushing out to choose either container or plants, do measure the space available to make sure that everything will fit. A stone box full of plants and compost will be heavy, so make sure the ledge or brackets will bear the weight. Consider how the box and plants will appear from the inside, as well as from the outside. Trailing plants will need to contrast with the building material of the walls. There is no use having red-coloured plants against red brick, or white against white-washed walls.

Our containers were chosen for their appearance and durability. Plastic boxes will be lighter, cheaper and, although not so pretty, can be concealed by trailing plants. Moisture retention will also be better in summer than with a terracotta box.

Remember, though, that attention to drainage will be important in winter so that plants are not waterlogged. The same rules apply as with any other kind of container. For the benefit of both plants and boxes, crock adequately and use a good compost, such as John Innes No. 2 or 3 with added peat and grit or a mixture of equal amounts of John Innes with a peat-based compost. Some of the peat-alternative composts look promising and I am sure more of us will be using them in the future.

Boxes are both narrower and shallower than most other kinds of container. Root run will be restricted and this will reflect on the plants that will thrive inside. Small bedding plants, patio roses, dwarf conifers and small evergreen shrubs will be the order of the day. The scale will suit a wide range of smaller spring bulbs which can be used in many combinations, either alone or mixed with other plants. The perusal of a comprehensive bulb catalogue alongside a list of other plants will provide inspiration for many more combinations than we have the space to show. Use small-growing spring-flowerers like primulas, white arabis, yellow *Allyssum saxatile* and aubretia as well as spring-bedding plants such as polyanthus, pansies, myosotis and bellis.

## PLANTS

1 Two hart's tongue ferns (*Phyllitis scolopendrium*).
2 One variegated thyme.
3 One dwarf yarrow (*Achillea tomentosa*).
4 One *Anthemis punctata cupaniana*.
5 One *Osteospermum ecklonis* 'Prostratum'.
6 One balm of Gilead (*Cedronella triphylla*).
7 Two shuttlecock ferns (*Matteuccia struthiopteris*).

**CONTAINER** Chilstone Regency Wall Trough measuring 23 inches (58.5 cm) long by 10 inches (25.5 cm) wide.

**POSITION** There should be sun for at least part of the day.

While some containers are planted for the general impact of shape and colour, others can be a wild, interesting assortment inviting closer inspection. This beautiful wall trough burgeons with an unusual choice of plants, some of which would have to be tracked down at specialist nurseries.

Planting time should be spring or early summer. Due to the half-hardy nature of cedronella and, to an extent, osteospermum, this container should not be stood outside until the end of May or early June. Crock the base well and half-fill the container loosely with John Innes No. 2 compost with added peat and grit or a mixture of equal amounts of John Innes No. 2 and a peat-based compost. Check watering regularly and liquid feed monthly with a well-balanced fertiliser from June onwards.

The dominant and most unusual plant, sending its long flower stems in all directions with abandon is *Cedronella triphylla*. A native of the Canary Islands, it has sweetly fragrant leaves when rubbed and interesting spikes of pinkish-purple flowers in July. If finding a plant proves difficult, they can be raised from seed (Chiltern Seeds *see page 122*). At the end of the season, lift and pot the plant, cut back by half, and overwinter in a frost-free greenhouse. A hard pruning in spring will see regeneration of flowering stems.

Most gardeners are familiar with the tall achillea or yarrow with large flat heads of yellow flower. *Achillea tomentosa* is a low-growing version often planted on rock gardens. Here, its soft, woolly leaves sit attractively on the edge of the trough. The daisy-like flowers of the osteopermum and anthemis look particularly good against a backdrop of ferns.

The hardy plants in the trough could be left indefinitely with a little judicious pruning, thinning and division to keep them under control. While the half-hardies enjoy a winter break in the greenhouse, their place could be taken by some well-chosen spring bulbs.

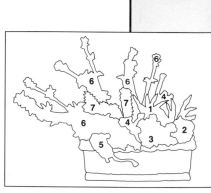

## PLANTS

1 Two dwarf conifers (*Thuja orientalis* 'Aurea Nana').
2 One *Euonymus fortunei* 'Emerald 'n' Gold.
3 Ten bulbs of *Crocus* 'Remembrance'.
4 Two double primrose (*Primula* 'Miss Indigo').
5 One variegated lesser periwinkle (*Vinca minor* 'Aureovariegata').
6 Fifteen bulbs of blue reticulata iris (*Iris* 'Joyce').

**CONTAINER** Trough from Lemon Green Landscapes measuring 31 inches (79 cm) long, 10 inches (25.5 cm) wide and 10 inches (25.5 cm) deep.

**POSITION** Sunny position preferred but shade tolerated.

**A** mixture of symmetry and informality can be most attractive in a window box. The neat, compact shape of the conifers is formal but not high enough to block light from the window. The other plants, chosen for evergreen foliage, variegated leaf colour, winter and spring flowers, simply fit in where they can.

Plant in the autumn, crocking the bottom of the trough well. Use John Innes No. 2 compost with added peat and grit or a mixture of equal amounts of John Innes No. 2 and a peat-based compost. Position the conifers, and then arrange the rest of the plants around them. Finally, add the bulbs, pushing them in between the plants so that the tips will be buried by about 2 inches (5 cm). Leave a good margin to allow for regular watering. Even after rain, a window box might be dry if sheltered by the building.

*Thuja orientalis* 'Aurea Nana' is ideal for a window box because it takes its time to reach an ultimate 2 feet (61 cm). The bright, yellow-green foliage turns bronze in winter and makes an excellent foil for the colour of winter and spring flowerers. Other permanent planting is provided by the trailing lesser periwinkle, which, as well as having evergreen, trailing foliage, bears bright blue flowers in summer. *E. fortunei* 'Emerald 'n' Gold' is better known as a low-growing ground cover plant but lends itself admirably to container planting. Undisturbed, well-watered and liquid-fed in summer, it will grow into a fine mound.

Any kind of primrose or polyanthus will be effective, but for containers why not make the effort and choose something a bit special. Named varieties of double primrose fit the bill exactly. There are many to choose from but most would have to be mail ordered from a specialist grower (*see page 122*). After flowering in late spring, remove the plants to a shady spot in the garden. Well looked after, they can be lifted in autumn or winter and used again. The bulbs, too, can be planted out in the garden but buy fresh ones for use in containers the following autumn.

By the end of May, having cleared out the spring-flowering plants, summer bedding can be added in amongst the permanent residents to give the window box a fresh lease of life.

### PLANTS

1 Two *Euonymus japonicus* 'Microphyllus Albovariegatus'.
2 Five pink hyacinths.
3 Four blue hyacinths.
4 Three double daisies (*Bellis perennis* 'Tasso Red').
5 Four winter/spring-flowering pansies.

**CONTAINER** Trough from Lemon Green Landscapes measuring 31 inches (79 cm) long, 10 inches (25.5 cm) wide and 10 inches (25.5 cm) deep.

**POSITION** A sunny position would be best but light shade is tolerated.

For a window box not to obscure the window it decorates, planting must be as low as possible while remaining in scale with the container. Here two euonymus stand like sentries, their closely packed, small leaves of interest all year round. To provide bright seasonal colour for winter and spring the pansies and bellis are planted between, with the thick, fragrant spikes of hyacinths pushing through. When all the spring flowers have finished, the plants can be replaced with summer bedding, leaving the euonymus in place.

Plant in autumn, crocking the base well. Use John Innes No. 2 compost with added peat and grit or a mixture of equal amounts of John Innes No. 2 and a peat-based compost. Position the euonymus first, then arrange the bellis and pansies around them, and finally push the hyacinth bulbs in amongst the root balls of the other plants so that their tips will be buried under about 2 inches (5 cm) of compost. Leave a good margin at the top for watering.

While these plants should be readily available from garden centres, the bellis and pansies can be grown from seed. This should be sown in June, after the mad rush of sowing and planting summer bedding. Apart from the obvious satisfaction of growing them, specific varieties can be chosen. Bellis mixtures are lovely because they are variations on the theme of white, pink and red which blend so well together. Either the large, fluffy-looking doubles or small pompon-like varieties would be suitable. Pansy 'Universal White' (Suttons Seeds) would be ideal but an alternative would be the pinks of 'Love Duet' or 'Imperial Pink Shades' (Mr Fothergill's).

Choice of hyacinth varieties can be personal. 'Pink Pearl' and 'Delft Blue' would be easily obtainable. A good plan is to plant a few hyacinths in individual 3½-inch (9-cm) pots in the autumn. Any old compost can be used and the pots simply covered with garden soil to insulate them from frost. These act as a contingency to add instant colour to the garden in spring or plant up a hasty window box at any time during winter or spring.

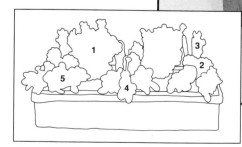

## PLANTS

1 Twenty bulbs of *Narcissus* 'Quince'.
2 Five pots or 20 bulbs of grape hyacinth (*Muscari armeniacum* 'Cantab').
3 Four yellow hybrid primroses.

**CONTAINER** Chilstone Regency Wall Trough measuring 23 inches (58.5 cm) long by 10 inches (25.5 cm) wide.

**POSITION** Sunny position preferred but semi-shade tolerated.

A most attractive mass of spring-flowering plants short enough not to obscure the window look wonderful in this grand trough. The possible combinations of bulbs are endless. Bear in mind other colours in view from inside the window, on curtains, for instance.

Plant up in the autumn, first crocking the base of the trough well. Begin filling with John Innes No. 2 compost with added peat and grit or a mixture of equal amounts of John Innes No. 2 and a peat-based compost. Arrange the primroses at the correct height in the front, then place the daffodil bulbs so that after filling in with compost, their tips will be covered by 1 to 2 inches (2.5 to 5 cm). After scattering some compost around them, add the grape hyacinth bulbs, then finish filling in with compost and firm down lightly, leaving enough room for watering. Check regularly to make sure the compost stays moist.

There are so many good small daffodils it is difficult to have favourites. Alternatives to 'Quince', a *cyclamineus* type, might include 'February Gold' from the same group. A daintier choice would be the delightful 'Hawera', a multi-headed *triandrus* hybrid with lemon-yellow flowers. In the *tazetta* group, another multi-headed daffodil, 'Minnow', is very pretty, having creamy white flowers with flattish lemon cups.

The ordinary wild primrose, *Primula vulgaris*, would look best of all planted at the front of dainty bulbs. For most colour impact, hybrid primroses or even polyanthus are the obvious choice. There are some great seed mixtures to choose from should you want to grow your own. Seed is best sown as fresh as possible, so don't delay the sowings. Try to germinate at 60°F (16°C) or below as the higher temperatures that some seeds prefer can induce dormancy.

When the spring display is finished, the planting is best dismantled to free the container for summer bedding. Lift the bulbs carefully, transferring them to a permanent spot in the garden. Likewise, plant the primroses in a shady spot. They can be used again for containers if lifted and cleaned during the following autumn, winter or spring.

## PLANTS

1 Six double-flowered primrose 'Ken Dearman'.
2 Four double-flowered primrose 'Sunshine Susie'.

**CONTAINER** Wavy Line Trough from Wichford Pottery measuring 22 inches (56 cm) long, 7 inches (18 cm) deep and 7 inches (18 cm) wide.

**POSITION** Not in full sun. This container is ideal for a north-facing position.

There is no need to feel that every container planted has to be a clever combination of many different types of plants. Simple groups of single subjects can be just as effective – for instance, one carefully chosen colour of spring-flowering pansies in a hanging basket, a mass of gold or red wallflowers in a large pot or this trough of double-flowered primroses.

The plants will probably have to be ordered through a specialist nursery, which will give you the chance to select which varieties you would like. The best planting time is January although autumn would be an alternative. John Innes No. 2 compost with added peat and grit or a mixture of equal amounts of John Innes No. 2 and a peat-based compost will be ideal. Make sure the base of the container is adequately crocked to ensure good drainage.

Double primroses are rather special plants which have been in and out of fashion as gardeners' favourites since Elizabethan times. Our trough was photographed in January but plants flower best in April and May. When they have finished, the best plan is to lift them out and plant in a shady border for the summer, releasing the trough for summer bedding plants. They should bulk up into good-sized clumps which can be lifted in January, split and planted back in the trough. Plants are perfectly hardy and seem to perform even better when they have experienced the contrast of a good cold winter.

Although not a strong perfume, a mass of primroses will produce a definite scent on a warm spring day which is barely discernible from one plant on its own. 'Ken Dearman' is one of my favourites with coppery orange flowers which combine to give a warm, glowing effect with 'Sunshine Susie' whose flowers really are a sunny yellow.

For earlier flowering, *Primula petiolaris* from the Himalayas is a good container plant which associates well with bulbs. This will prefer an acid compost and a shady position. Auriculas are another group for a trough but beware, you might be bitten by the bug for collecting them.

### Stockist
Craven's Nursery, Hall Barn Nurseries, Windsor End, Beaconsfield, Bucks HP9 2SG.

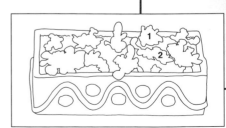

### PLANTS

1 Three white petunias.
2 Three pale pink petunias.
3 Four *Helichrysum petiolare.*

**CONTAINER** Terracotta trough from Secret Garden measuring 31 inches (79 cm) long and 6½ inches (16.5 cm) wide.

**POSITION** Full sun or sun for most of the day.

Petunias are such good plants for window boxes and troughs that it is difficult not to use them again and again. However, rather than just massing lots of colours together it is worth considering a gentle combination of white and pink flowers with the silver foliage of helichrysum. Here, the flowers of pale yellow add their own soft colour to the arrangement.

As these plants are tender they should not be placed outside until late May or early June. Crock the base of the trough well. Compost should be John Innes No. 2 with added peat and sharp sand or alternatively a mixture of equal amounts of John Innes and a peat-based potting compost. Allow room at the top for watering. Keep moist throughout summer and liquid-feed weekly with a high-nitrogen fertiliser at first, changing to high-potash for better flowering. Dead-head the petunias regularly to help them produce a succession of flowers.

Petunias are very easy to grow from seed, germinating at about 65°F (18°C) in a propagating case or in the house. Transfer the germinated seedlings to a frost-free greenhouse and grow on, pricking out when large enough to handle. This gives you the opportunity to choose your own varieties. 'Super Cascade Blush Improved' (Thompson and Morgan) is a good pink and could be combined with 'Resisto Pure White' (Dobies) or 'Supermagic White' (Suttons). However, separate plants in pots are available from garden centres, where hopefully you can pick out the colours you need. Helichrysum is easier to buy each year. Cuttings can be struck during summer and over-wintered in a frost-free greenhouse. However, they are not always easy to root, tending to rot if their furry leaves become too moist and warm.

For a change, white and pink verbena could be used, or try combining blue and white petunias or blue and white verbena with silver foliage. Short-growing nicotiana (tobacco plants) like the 'Roulette' or 'Domino' strains would also be suitable although rather upright in growth. Their main advantage is that they are tolerant of dull, wet summers.

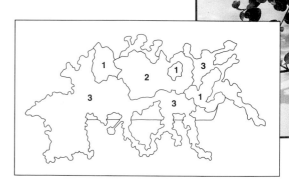

## PLANTS

1 Four white tobacco plants (*Nicotiana affinis*).
2 Four dark blue petunias.
3 Two *Helichrysum petiolare*.
4 One large *Convolvulus sabatius* (formerly *C. mauritanicus*).

**CONTAINER** Haddonstone Belton Trough measuring 34 inches (86.5 cm) long by 15 inches (38 cm) wide, by 11½ inches (29 cm) high.

**POSITION** Full sun.

**D**istinguished rather than colourful, this container is planted with a subtle combination of white, silvery grey and blue. The grey stone of the trough and the colour of the plants would lend a cool effect to a hot, sunny corner.

Plant in the spring but as the plants are tender they should not be placed outside until late May or early June. Crock well, then use a John Innes compost with added peat or grit or a mixture of equal amounts of John Innes No. 2 and a peat-based compost. Once the plants have started to grow, give a couple of liquid feeds with a well-balanced or high-nitrogen fertiliser. After this, swap to a fortnightly feed with a high-potash fertiliser. Both this and regular dead-heading will ensure a succession of flowers.

Nicotiana are easily raised from spring-sown seed. The taller types are the ones that have the best fragrance but if the box is intended for a windowsill, it might become impossible to see out. Most suitable would be 'Domino White' which, although not very scented, only grows to about 1 foot (30 cm) and has its flowers well open all day. Petunias are easy to raise from seed. Dark purple/blue is represented by 'Resisto Blue' from Dobies or Unwins Seeds. Helichrysum is freely available in garden centres and can be propagated from summer cuttings. If you should take helichrysum cuttings, don't enclose them in plastic or polythene, otherwise the moist atmosphere will rot their felty leaves and shoots.

*Convolvulus sabatius*, from North Africa, is a trailing perennial which should open its blue-purple flowers all summer and into autumn. Once you have found a plant (*see stockist below*), it can be propagated by summer cuttings. At the end of the summer, when the container is emptied, the parent plant could be risked outside in a well-drained border. Plants should survive mild winters but try to keep young specimens enjoying frost-free protection in reserve.

### Stockist

Hopleys Plants Ltd, High Street, Much Hadham, Herts SG10 6BU.

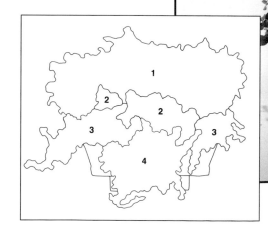

## PLANTS

**1** Two pink marguerites
   (*Argyranthemum* 'Petite Pink').
**2** Three white tuberous begonias.
**3** Four *Verbena × hybrida* 'Sissinghurst'.

**CONTAINER** Wavy Line Trough from
Wichford Pottery measuring 22 inches
(56 cm) long by 7 inches (18 cm) wide.

**POSITION** Full sun.

This bright terracotta box needs striking,
warm-coloured flowers and these are
amply supplied by the profusion of almost
shocking-pink blooms from *Verbena*
'Sissinghurst'. This tones down through
the pale pink of the argyranthemum to the
white of the begonias, giving a real 'hot
box' feel to the whole arrangement. Well
suited to a windowsill, the plants will not
grow too tall, while a display of verbena
flowers will trail over the front all summer.

Plant up in spring but do not stand outside until late May or early June as the
plants are not hardy. Crock the base well
and use a compost of John Innes No. 2
with added peat and sharp sand or a mixture of John Innes No. 2 and a peat-based
compost. Once they are established, start
feeding with a well-balanced liquid feed
every week. As the summer progresses,
change to a high-potash feed to give a good
boost to flowering potential. Dead-head
regularly to keep new flowers forming.

Argyranthemum and verbena will have
to be bought in at least for their first year.
Once you have stock, summer cuttings can
be rooted to overwinter as small plants to
use the following year. Tuberous begonias,
usually of the 'Nonstop' variety, can be
bought in as tubers and started into
growth in a warm place or grown from seed
which is usually sold in mixed colours, so
picking out white-flowered plants from
the garden centre might be a safer bet. At
the end of the summer, take the plants out
of the container, pot up until they die
down, then store the tubers frost-free until
the following year. Once the container has
finished it can be dismantled and filled
with plants for winter and spring interest.

There are many alternatives to consider
which will complement this warm terracotta. If there is room for more height, a
taller pink argyranthemum with larger
flower size and, therefore, more impact,
would be A. 'Vancouver'. In recent seasons I have noticed ranunculus for sale in
garden centres, their rounded flowers
looking as if they have been made out of
tissue paper. Allyssum planted between
the verbena would make startling patches
of white amongst the pink flowers.

Bright pansies, pink dianthus, warm-
coloured patio roses and perhaps a golden
heather or two for bright foliage would be
another worthy combination.

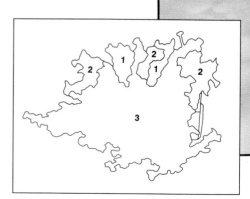

## PLANTS

**1** One yellow miniature rose (*Rosa* 'Guernsey Gold').

**2** Two white marguerites (*Argyranthemum frutescens*).

**3** Three golden helichrysum (*Helichrysum petiolare* 'Limelight').

**CONTAINER** Stone window box from Knollys Nursery measuring 36 inches (91.5 cm) long by 12 inches (30.5 cm) wide.

**POSITION** Full sun or sun for most of the day.

There is something cool and pleasant about this combination of yellow miniature rose with lime-green helichrysum and the small white daisy-like flowers of the marguerite. A fairly tall planting for a window box, it would be suitable for a deep window or perhaps just to stand down by the side of a front door.

Plant up in the spring. As only the rose is hardy, the plants should not be stood outside before late May or early June. Crock well, then use a compost created by mixing equal quantities of John Innes No. 2 with a peat-based compost. All these plants should be available from garden centres as reasonably large specimens for a good instant effect. However, with regular watering and weekly liquid feeds of well-balanced fertiliser, even small plants will soon knit together. Dead-head regularly throughout summer to encourage a succession of flowers.

Patio roses and miniatures like this 'Guernsey Gold' make delightful additions to troughs and window boxes as they are mostly compact, bushy small plants. Repeat flowering is one of their valued characteristics. *Argyranthemum frutescens* is a native of the Canary Islands. Having invested in the plants, it is possible to take summer cuttings which, overwintered frost-free, can be used the following year. The same could be said for the helichrysum. These can be difficult to root and prefer not to be covered by plastic or polythene as their soft, felty leaves might rot. When the container is dismantled in autumn, I would pot up the rose and keep it for the next year. Alternatively, leave the rose in place, filling in the gaps around it with plants for winter and spring interest. Prune as you would a bush rose in March. The marguerites could be potted and would continue to flower for a while in a greenhouse or conservatory.

A white, red and gold box using a row of marguerites at the back, fronted with yellow summer pansies like the brilliant 'Imperial Gold Princess' from Unwins or 'Flame Princess' from Thompson and Morgan, which have red 'faces', would be a bright alternative. The front row could be a mixture of helichrysum and red lobelia.

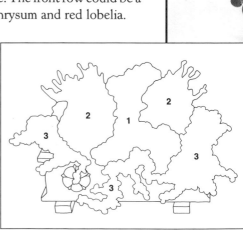

### PLANTS

1 One yellow miniature rose (*Rosa* 'Guernsey Gold').
2 Two cherry pies (*Heliotropium* 'Princess Marina').
3 Four pale yellow gazania.
4 Two yellow-leaved helichrysum (*Helichrysum petiolare* 'Limelight').
5 Two golden variegated ivies.

**CONTAINER** Sandstone trough from Knollys Nursery measuring 24 inches (61 cm) long by 10 inches (25.5 cm) wide.

**POSITION** Full sun.

This trough has been planted with an attractive, unusual and striking mixture of plants with purple and gold as the colour theme. Patio and miniature roses are ideal for containers as they make compact, bushy plants which reliably repeat-flower over a long period. Few would grow tall enough to create problems by blocking the view out of the window. Here, cherry pie or heliotrope will enrich the air with their sweet fragrance. A sunny spot will keep all the plants compact with bright foliage and a succession of flowers. Sun is particularly necessary for the flowers of the gazania to open fully.

Plant up in spring. As all the plants except the rose and ivy are tender, wait until late May or early June before placing outside. Crock well, then add John Innes No. 2 with extra peat and sharp sand or a mixture of equal amounts of John Innes No. 2 and a peat-based compost. After planting, leave a good margin at the top for watering. Once the plants are established, liquid-feed fortnightly with a well-balanced fertiliser. Dead-head regularly to encourage plenty of new buds.

Heliotropes should be widely available from garden centres or one can buy seed such as 'Dwarf Marine' and 'Hybrid Marine'. Sow early and grow on in pots as plants can take their time to flower. Once gazanias have been bought, these can be propagated very easily but must be overwintered frost-free. When the plants are removed from the container in autumn, simply cut small crowns of growth apart from the main plant. You will find that clumps of leaves are held together by short stems. Trim the long leaves so that they will not flop over and insert the short stems into cutting compost to root. Helichrysum can be propagated for the following year but is easily obtained in spring.

In autumn I would pot the roses and ivies for use another year but if you are short of space, they could be left in place and the gaps filled with plants for winter and spring interest.

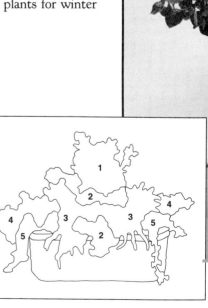

### PLANTS

1 One crimson annual or Japanese pink (*Dianthus*).
2 Two bright yellow French marigolds.
3 Two *Pelargonium* 'Silipen'.
4 Two red petunias.
5 Two golden heathers (*Erica carnea* 'Aurea').

**CONTAINER** Acanthus Window Box from Secret Garden Centre measuring 20 inches (51 cm) long by 8 inches (20 cm) wide.

**POSITION** Full sun.

This container planted with brightly coloured flowers and bolstered by the foliage of pelargoniums and ericas makes no pretensions at subtlety of colours. Red and bright yellow is the theme but shape is important too, the planting reaching an apex with the dianthus in the middle.

Plant in spring but do not stand outside until all danger of frost is past. Once in place, the plants will grow quickly and soon cheer up even the dullest building. Crock the base for good drainage. John Innes No. 2 compost with added peat and sharp sand or a mixture of equal amounts of John Innes No. 2 and a peat-based compost will suit the plants. Once the plants are established, begin weekly liquid feeds. Start with two high in nitrogen to boost growth, then switch to high-potash (like a tomato fertiliser) to promote flowering. Dead-head often to ensure a good succession of fresh flowers.

For those who like to raise their own plants from seed, the breeding of annual dianthus has seen much emphasis on dwarf, bushy plants for bedding purposes. The 'Princess' strain is suitable ('Princess Scarlet' from Suttons) but, failing this, the 'Knight Series' of carnations might be a good alternative ('Crimson Knight' from Suttons). There are many marigolds to choose from. 'Disco Marietta' (Suttons), a dwarf single French, is a sunny combination of gold and yellow with deep mahogany blotches. At 6 inches (15 cm) tall it will not compete with the dianthus. Finding a good red petunia should not be a problem. 'Supermagic Red' from Suttons is a grandiflora which does grow quite tall but should sprawl outwards. 'Ruby Cascade' from Thompson and Morgan is particularly suitable for pouring out of a container. However, if growing lots of seed for just one or two plants is too much of an effort, then plants can easily be obtained from garden centres.

*Pelargonium* 'Silipen' is a semi-double with red flowers but is planted here for its wonderfully compact, rounded foliage. Golden heathers bristle out from beneath to give compact shape to the arrangement.

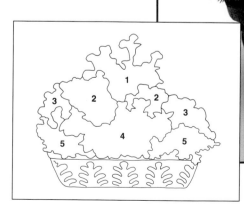

### PLANTS

1 Four red tuberous begonias.
2 Six Swedish ivy (*Plectranthus coleoides* 'Marginatus').

**CONTAINER** Chilstone Regency Wall Trough measuring 23 inches (58.5 cm) long by 10 inches (25.5 cm) wide.

**POSITION** Sun or semi-shade but must be sheltered.

There is no reason why one has to stick to conventional bedding plants to achieve summer colour. They are reliable but why not take a chance and go for foliage colour as striking as this plectranthus? A lot of small flowers would create a confused effect, so combine it with the bold flowers of red tuberous begonias.

As neither of these plants are hardy, they should not be stood outside until early June. The plectranthus, usually grown as a houseplant, must have a sheltered spot out of cold winds for it to flourish all summer outdoors. Crock the base of the trough to assist drainage. A peat-based or peat-alternative compost would suit both plants. By mid-June, plants will benefit from a weekly, well-balanced liquid feed. Dead-head the begonias to ensure a good continuation of flowers. There is a danger of overwatering the plectranthus so never swamp the compost, though do keep it moist.

Tuberous begonias bought from the garden centre are usually of the 'Nonstop' variety. These have flowers 2 to 3 inches (5 to 8 cm) across, produced all summer in great profusion on compact plants about 12 inches (30 cm) tall. Seed of these is tiny which makes raising them at home a skilled job. At the end of the season, plants can be lifted and potted, dried off, then the tubers rested until the following year. Pull off the old roots, then plant hollow side up in peat or compost during March, keep warm and they will soon sprout.

Plectranthus can be propagated at any time throughout the summer by taking off short tip cuttings. Pot three to a small pot and they will soon fill it. The old plants, when removed from the container well before cold autumn weather starts, make excellent trailing pot or hanging basket plants for house or conservatory.

Should you be put off using a 'houseplant' in an outdoor container, then try a compact and brightly variegated ivy which could be left out all year round. Even tolerant of shade it could be teamed with red impatiens for a similar effect on a north-facing aspect. Any bright bedding plant with large flowers like red petunias or red salvia could be substituted for the begonia.

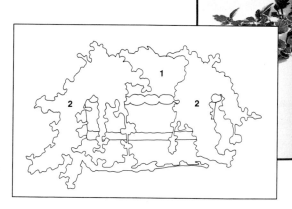

## CONTAINERS WERE BORROWED FROM:

Bentinck Nurseries, Send Dip, Ripley, Surrey.

Bryans Garden Centre, 100 Tooting Bec Road, London SW17

Chilstone Architectural Ornaments, Sprivers, Horsmonden, Tonbridge, Kent TN12 8DR.

Andrew Crace Designs, Bourne Lane, Much Hadham, Herts SG10 6ER.

Knollys Nursery, Knollys Road, Streatham, London SW16 2JH.

Haddonstone Ltd, The Forge House, East Haddon, Northampton NN6 8DB.

Lemon Green Landscapes, 21 Lendel Terrace, Clapham North, London.

Pamal, The Cottage, Sproxton, Melton Mowbray, Leics LE14 4QS.

Rockinghams Garden Centre, Waddon Way, Croydon.

Secret Garden, Westow Street, Upper Norwood, London SE19.

Wetheriggs Country Pottery, Clifton Dykes, Penrith, Cumbria CA10 2DH.

Wichford Pottery, Wichford, Shipston-on-Stour, Warks CV36 5PG.

## PLANTS WERE BORROWED FROM:

Anglo Aquarium Plant Co. Ltd, Strayfield Road, Enfield, Middx EN2 9JE.

Barnsdale Plants, Exton Avenue, Exton, Oakham, Rutland LE15 8AH.

Blackhorse Nursery, Blackhorse Road, Worplesdon, Woking, Surrey.

Coblands Nursery Ltd, Trench Road, Tonbridge, Kent TN10 3HQ.

Fords Container Stock Ltd, Carthouse Lane Nurseries, Horsell, Woking, Surrey GU21 4XS (suppliers of extra-large plants).

Higgs and Sons Ltd, Castle Grove Nursery, Scotts Grove Road, Chobham, Woking, Surrey GU24 8DY.

Hopley's Plants, Much Hadham, Herts SG10 6BU.

North Hill Nurseries, Scots Grove Road, Chobham, Surrey GU24 8DW.

Rockinghams Garden Centre, Waddon Way, Croydon.

Round Pond Nurseries, Chobham Place, Chobham, Nr Woking, Surrey GU24 8TW.

## SEED COMPANIES MENTIONED IN BOOK:

Chiltern Seeds, Bortree Stile, Ulverston, Cumbria LA12 7PB.

Samuel Dobie and Son Ltd, Broomhill Way, Torquay, Devon TQ2 7QW.

Mr Fothergill's Seeds Ltd, Kentford, Newmarket, Suffolk CB8 7QB.

Suttons Seeds Ltd, Hele Road, Torquay, Devon TQ2 7QJ.

Thompson and Morgan, London Road, Ipswich, Suffolk IP2 0BA.

Unwins Seeds Ltd, Histon, Cambridge CB4 4LE.

# INDEX